Charles Henry Sargant

Urban Rating

Being an Inquiry into the Incidence of local Taxation in Towns....

Charles Henry Sargant

Urban Rating

Being an Inquiry into the Incidence of local Taxation in Towns....

ISBN/EAN: 9783337113056

Printed in Europe, USA, Canada, Australia, Japan

Cover: Foto ©Suzi / pixelio.de

More available books at **www.hansebooks.com**

URBAN RATING

BEING

AN INQUIRY INTO THE INCIDENCE OF

LOCAL TAXATION IN TOWNS

WITH SPECIAL REFERENCE TO CURRENT PROPOSALS

FOR CHANGE.

BY

CHARLES HENRY SARGANT,

OF NEW COLLEGE, OXFORD, M.A.

AND OF LINCOLN'S INN, BARRISTER-AT-LAW.

LONDON

LONGMANS, GREEN, AND CO
AND NEW YORK: 15 EAST 16th STREET
1890.

PREFACE.

In a little book published in the spring of 1886, and entitled "Ground-Rents and Building-Leases," I endeavoured to deal with two questions which were then beginning to occupy the attention of a Select Committee of the House of Commons, namely, "Leasehold Enfranchisement" and "The Rating of Ground-Rents." With regard to Leasehold Enfranchisement, I there pointed out many of the more obvious objections to the current proposals on the subject, above all that the result would be to enfranchise not the occupier but the middleman; and showed how hardly any such scheme would press on the prudent investor of moderate means. But to the rating of ground-rents I offered a still more decided and determined opposition, both as involving an unprecedented breach of the most deliberate contracts, and as throwing a burden on one class of the community to secure benefits to another class.

Since the appearance of my little work, the Select Committee of the House of Commons, which sat on through the Session of 1886 and was re-appointed in the Sessions of 1887, 1888, and 1889, has issued a report on the subject of Leasehold Enfranchisement, which substantially endorses both my conclusions and my reasoning on that question. But though considerable evidence was taken by the Committee upon the rating of ground-rents, and on the cognate subject of the rating of vacant building land—or, to adopt the precise terms of the reference, on "the " question of imposing a direct assessment on the " owners of ground-rents, and on the owners of in- " creased values imparted to land by building opera- " tions or other improvements "—the Committee have not yet thought fit to make any report on this head, but have recommended their own further re-appointment with the view of collecting additional evidence.

Under these circumstances I have been urged by certain gentlemen with large interests in urban building land to re-state in more detail, and with the greater experience which I have since acquired on the subject, the considerations which had previously led me to condemn the current proposals to rate ground-rents; and the following pages are the result. I have felt no difficulty in complying with this request, because since the writing of my book I have devoted much attention and reflection to the subject and have carefully studied the whole of the evidence given before the Select Committee of the House of Commons, and much else that has appeared in print ; and this study and reflection have only strengthened the convictions which I had previously entertained, and had expressed in my book, before I had any professional connection with the question.

I am afraid that no treatment of the subject can render it other than a dry and repulsive one, perhaps the driest and most repulsive of all that statesmen have to deal with. But, after all, real politics are serious work. And in this case the more the question is studied the larger appear the interests involved, and the greater therefore the necessity of arriving at an accurate and dispassionate judgment.

C. H. S.

Lincoln's Inn :
    March 1890.

CONTENTS.

	PAGE
CHAPTER I.—THE ORIGIN AND NATURE OF GROUND-RENTS	7
,, II.—THE DETERMINATION OF GROUND-RENT ...	25
,, III.—HAVE GROUND-RENTS ALREADY PAID RATES?	36
,, IV.—THE PROPOSALS TO RATE GROUND-RENTS	55
,, V.—RATING AS BETWEEN BUILDING-OWNER AND OCCUPIER	71
,, VI.—RATING BETWEEN BUILDING-OWNERS AND OWNERS OF FIXED RENTS ...	90
,, VII.—RATING BETWEEN BUILDING-OWNERS AND THE OWNERS OF REVERSIONS	110
,, VIII.—THE RATING OF VACANT BUILDING LAND	127
,, IX.—GENERAL REMARKS AND CONCLUSION ...	146
APPENDIX	159

[NOTE.—The references in the margin are, except when otherwise stated, to the evidence given before the Select Committee on Town Holdings during the Sessions of 1886, 1887, and 1888, which is a mine of wealth on all questions connected with building land.]

URBAN RATING.

CHAPTER I.

THE ORIGIN AND NATURE OF GROUND-RENTS.

To the lawyer, surveyor, or land agent, or to any other person having a professional acquaintance with building land, it will appear a waste of time to inquire into the origin or characteristics of ground-rents. But in a layman, however well informed on most subjects, it is extremely rare to find anything like an accurate knowledge of the subject; and without an accurate knowledge of what a ground-rent really is and how it has originated, it is quite impossible to enter into any profitable discussion of how it should be treated from the point of view of taxation. While, therefore, it will be open to all professional readers to pass by this chapter unread, for almost all others it will be advisable to give their closest attention to its contents.

When suburban land gradually comes into the building market it is very rarely indeed that the landowner possesses the capital and the special knowledge required for the erection of houses; and, this being so, he is in general compelled to dispose of it to some other person for the purpose. On this disposition the consideration received by the landowner may take either of two distinct forms. He may either sell his land, or such part of it as is from

<small>Position of owner of building land.</small>

time to time required, for a lump sum or a succession of lump sums payable either immediately or by instalments. Or he may take his price in the shape of periodical payments of the nature of interest on the capital value of the land, such payments being in general calculated annually and made at half-yearly or quarterly intervals. The first of these two methods of payment constitutes what is conveniently called the "freehold purchase system" of building, and is perhaps the most widely prevalent of all the systems of building in vogue in England. The second method, which is also extensively adopted, especially where the value of land is high and it would be difficult for the builder to provide its capital value, is practised in several different forms, of which the most important are (*a*) the "freehold rent-charge system," which is practically equivalent to the Scotch system of "feu" rents, (*b*) the 999 years system, and (*c*) the 99 years system. About these three different methods some words of explanation must be given.

<small>Methods of hiring out building land.</small> It is obvious that a landowner who is hiring out his land for a periodical payment may so hire it out either (1) for the whole duration of his own estate, that is for ever, if he is the owner of the fee simple, or (2) for a term of years practically, though not theoretically, equivalent to a fee simple, such as the ordinary term of 999 years,* or (3) for a term of years bearing some relation to the probable duration of the buildings to be erected, such as the terms of 200 and 150 years usual in Dublin or the ordinary London term of 99

---

* Instances were mentioned before the Select Committee on Town Holdings of leases, or 10,000 and 20,000 years in Ireland and for 5,000 years at Truro.

years. Now, according to the law of England, a landowner who disposes of his land for the *whole* duration of his estate is unable to create any *tenure* between himself and the person who deals with him, and is unable therefore to reserve any *rent* strictly so called, since rent is only one of the incidents of tenure. Rent can only be reserved if the landowner parts with something less in point of duration than his whole estate in the land, so that he has left what is called a *reversion*—that is, some period of time of whatever length at the commencement of which the land will *revert* or come back to him on the expiration of the lesser estate which he has granted away.*

Whenever then an English landowner is minded in accordance with a custom in the locality, or for any other reason, to grant land for ever for building purposes in consideration of a periodical payment, he does not attempt to reserve a *rent*, but limits to himself a rent-charge of the agreed amount, with special provisions (now given by statute) for securing its payment. And from this time forth he is considered in law not as having any *estate* whatever in the *land* (which would be the case if he had granted a lease for however long a period, short of the

_{The freehold rent-charge system.}

* It may be well to note here that when a landowner has once made a grant of a lesser estate than his own, reserving a rent, this rent at once becomes *incident to* and follows the reversion. Laymen often fall into the mistake of talking of the ground-rent reserved on a building lease and the reversion expectant on its termination as two different and separable things. For the purposes of calculation it may often be advisable to separate the two, since, as will be seen later on, the rent payable during the currency of a lease is often no measure whatever of the value of the reversion. But as a matter of fact the two form one inseparable whole and are always conveyed together. A "freehold ground-rent" *includes* the reversion in fee simple on the termination of the lease. A "leasehold ground-rent" also includes a reversion, though generally only a nominal reversion of a day or two.

duration of his own estate), but as merely entitled to a rent-charge issuing out of the land. And this system of payment, or development for building purposes, is conveniently known as the "freehold rent-charge system," while the rent-charges created under it are often (though inaccurately) known in Manchester and other places where the system is prevalent as "chief-*rents*." In Scotland a difference of law allows landowners, while granting away their land for ever, to create a tenure between themselves and the grantees and to reserve a perpetual periodical payment of the nature of rent. These payments are generally known as "feu-duties" and the system as that of "feuing."

The building-lease system.

On the other hand, should the custom of the locality be to grant land for building purposes for 999 years (as in many of the principal Lancashire towns), or for 99 years (as in London and Birmingham), the landowner *leases* the land to the builder for the agreed number of years, reserving to himself a *rent* of the required amount, and having obviously left in himself a reversion in the land (to which the rent is incident) after the expiration of the term of years which he has granted. And whether the term so granted be 999 years or 99 years, or indeed whether it be 10,000 years or 1 year, the landowner is alike considered in law as having the immediate freehold estate in the land, subject only to the lease. It is, however, obvious that, although in all its legal incidents the 999 years system is precisely analogous to the 99 years system, yet for the practical purposes of valuation it far more closely resembles the freehold rent-charge or Scotch feuing system. For a reversion to occur at the end of 999 years is absolutely worthless, and the interest of the landowner therefore *practically* only consists in a perpetual annual payment, as under either of the two last-mentioned systems. But a reversion to occur at the end of 99 years, if it has no actual present value, is at any rate within a "measurable distance" of acquiring such a value in the future, the evidence of experts being that the reversionary value will begin to make itself felt in some 20 or 30 years.

Tewson (1887), 3,058. Castle (1887), 7,357.

Such, then, are the four principal methods by which in England land is covered with houses, namely, (1) the freehold-purchase system, under which the builder buys the land out and out for a lump sum or a succession of lump sums; (2) the freehold rent-charge system (nearly equivalent to the Scotch system of feuing), under which the builder buys the land for a recurring annual payment which is charged on the land and house as a yearly rent-charge; (3) the 999 years or long leasehold system, under which the builder pays for the land by a periodical annual payment called rent, and takes a lease of land and house at this rent for a long and practically inexhaustible term of years; and (4) the 99 years or London leasehold system, under which the builder also obtains only a lease of the land and house, and that for a comparatively short or measurable period, and at a rent which is in fact slightly lower than under either of the two last-mentioned systems, on account of the smaller estate obtained by the builder, and the reversionary value which will soon begin to belong to the landowner. It is no part of the scope of this work to treat of any less usual systems of building, such as that of leases for lives or for terms of years dependent on

General review of building systems.

lives, nor to enter into any comparison of the relative advantages and disadvantages of the four more usual methods. Indeed, if a landowner always dealt with a wealthy builder for a single site fronting on a high road properly made and sewered, a sufficient account for the purposes of these pages would already have been given of the methods under which houses are built and paid for and ground-rents and annual payments of the like nature are created. But, as a matter of fact, no one of these three conditions is generally present. As a rule, builders need to raise all the capital they can procure. Considerable areas of land, or at any rate sites for several houses, are comprised in each transaction by the landowner, and roads and sewers have to be made for purposes of access and drainage; and thus considerable complications are introduced into what would otherwise be a simple and readily intelligible transaction.

The freehold purchase system at work.

Spain (1888), 8,736 et seq.

A typical instance of the actual development of building land on the freehold purchase system was brought before the Select Committee on Town Holdings from an estate at Newcastle-on-Tyne. The witness (Mr. Spain) says, that whenever any portion of the estate is required for building, the land is laid out by the vendor according to a ground-plan which is submitted to and approved by the sanitary authority; that builders apply for blocks or for individual sites; that in the case of large blocks they are sold to the builder or purchaser of the houses as the case may be, and he undertakes to pay for the roads and sewers, which are constructed in accordance with plans previously agreed on; that the builder also agrees to build a certain specified class of house of a specified maximum value; that on taking up his agreement in the case of larger blocks he pays 10 per cent. of the purchase-money, and agrees to pay the balance and complete his purchase by a day named, and failing that to pay interest at 4 per cent. for, say, the first two years, and 5 per cent. thereafter; and that the small builders pay no deposit, but in lieu of deposit pay at so much per yard super., *the price thus paid being larger than the wholesale price paid by the purchasers for larger blocks.* In other cases, as at Nottingham and Wolverhampton, the landowner is paid at once, and the necessary capital, or the bulk of it, is provided by some financial agent or mortgagee. The important points to be noticed are that even under the freehold-purchase system a large proportion of the price has to be provided by the landowner or some third party, and that the roads and sewers are directly or indirectly paid for by the landowner, not by the public.

Johnson (1888), 12,737.
Brevitt (1888), 1,846-7.

The actual method of development under the freehold rent-charge system, as practised at Bristol, has been described by Mr. Josiah Thomas, the city surveyor. The owner first makes the roads and sewers in accordance with the requirements of the local authority, and then lets the plots on these perpetual rent-charges. The builder cannot in general afford to pay a lump sum for the purchase of the land, and in order to get money for his buildings he is usually financed by or through the agency of the landowner; while to further facilitate his operations the rent-charge does not begin to grow payable till from some six to eighteen months after he has begun to build. Here again it is clear that the roads and sewers are provided by the landowner, and that, although the builder has not to borrow for the pur-

The freehold rent-charge system at work.

Josiah Thomas (1888), 3,116-22.

chase of his land, since that is provided for him at an annual payment, he has nevertheless to be helped by postponing the period when this annual payment first begins to accrue. Under this system also, as practised in Manchester and some other towns, a considerable tract will sometimes be taken by a land speculator at one entire rent-charge, and he will then, after forming roads and sewers, let off smaller plots at separate rent-charges, which in the aggregate exceed the amount of the first rent-charge. His profit will then be derived from the sale of the difference between the rent-charges he has to receive and that which he has to pay, such differences being popularly described as " second chief-rents." These second chief-rents obviously represent not any original land value, but simply and solely expenditure upon land ; and in this and other respects they are analogous to the " improved " or " leasehold " ground-rents, which will be dealt with shortly.

<small>The Scotch "feu" system at work.</small>

An exactly similar process seems to take place under the Scotch system of feuing, and a rather complicated transaction of the kind is described in the following passage from a pamphlet entitled " Should Feu-Duties be Taxed?" *

" We shall suppose that A, the proprietor
" of a building estate, feus five acres of that
" estate to B for an annual feu-duty of £150,
" being at the rate of £30 per acre. B prepares
" a feuing or building plan of the ground, and
" marks out roads and streets. B then sub-feus
" to C one acre of the ground thus laid out for

* By " Vindex." Edinburgh : David Douglas ; Glasgow : James Maclehose & Son ; London : Hamilton, Adams & Co. The whole pamphlet is lucidly written, and will well repay a careful study.

ORIGIN AND NATURE OF GROUND-RENTS. 15

" building, at a feu-duty of £40. C erects five
" villas, each on one-fifth of an acre, and sells
" the villas, each with its one-fifth of an acre of
" ground, imposing upon each a feu-duty of £10
" in addition to the cash price paid for the villas.
" The purchasers from C, viz., D, E, F, G, and
" H, are then each the proprietor of one-fifth
" of an acre of ground, with the villa thereon,
" subject to an annual payment of £10 to C.
" We shall further assume that the remaining
" four acres have been sub-feued and treated in
" a similar way, but it will only be necessary
" here to follow the history of the one acre we
" have noticed. A, in respect of that one acre,
" receives £30 a year from B. B, in respect of
" the same ground, receives £40 from C, and
" hands £30 to A, the difference of £10 per
" annum being B's profit on the transaction,
" and representing payment for his trouble in
" superintending the laying out of the ground.
" In the case we have put, the expense of making
" roads and drains is borne by the builder, C.
" Had B constructed the roads and drains he
" would have imposed a larger feu-duty on the
" ground when conveying it to C, in order to
" recoup his outlay, and the case would have
" been rendered more complex by that con-
" sideration. We shall take the simple case
" where C has borne the cost of roads and
" drains, and added the amount to the price of
" the villas. C, in selling his houses, endeavours
" to get a price that will repay his whole out-
" lay and leave him a profit. Part of the price
" is paid in the shape of a feu-duty, but by

"much the larger part is paid down. In the case stated the feu-duty imposed by C upon each of the five villa properties is £10, making £50 for the five, and as C only pays a feu-duty of £40, he has an annual profit of £10."

<small>The 999 years system.</small> No detailed separate account need be given of the covering of land with houses under the 999 years system, inasmuch as it is in substantial accordance with the process under the 99 years system, which will be described at some length in the succeeding paragraphs. The building is generally regulated by a preliminary agreement, which defines the character of the houses to be built, and entitles the builder, on their completion, to take up leases of the houses at the stipulated rent or rents. As under the other systems, the roads and sewers are either directly constructed by the landowner or undertaken by his lessees under arrangements made with him. And in this case also the expenditure of an original lessee upon development may be represented by the excess of the derivative rents which he can charge sub-lessees from him over the original rent which he has agreed to pay the proprietor of the fee simple.

<small>The 99 years system at work.</small> A more careful examination must be made of the development of land under the 99 years or London leasehold system. The general nature of the transaction appears to be accurately described in the following paragraph* from the draft report submitted for adoption to the Select Committee on Town Holdings by Mr. Knowles:—

"Accounts of the development of land under

---

* Paragraph 28, page 105 of the Report of the Select Committee, 1889.

" the building-lease or London leasehold system
" are given as to London by Mr. Ryde, Mr.
" Gregory, and Mr. Garrard, and as to Birming-
" ham by Mr. Mathews. It appears that the
" general practice is to enter into a preliminary
" agreement for the erection by the builder of
" one or more houses, and for the grant to him,
" when such erection is completed to the satis-
" faction of the landowner's surveyor, of a lease
" or leases at a total agreed ground-rent. When
" a small plot is let the roads have generally
" been previously made by the landowner; but
" in the case of larger pieces of land the lessee
" often agrees to make the roads and sewers,
" paying in that case a much smaller ground-
" rent. The total ground-rent is apportioned
" separately on the houses as they are built,
" the custom often being to secure on the houses
" first built more than their proportionate
" ground-rent, so that towards the conclusion
" of the operations the lessee will often be
" entitled to take up leases of the houses last built
" at a peppercorn or other nominal ground-rent.
" During the process of building the builder is
" accommodated by being charged only a pepper-
" corn rent, or in the case of considerable blocks
" of land a gradually increasing rent as houses
" are expected to be built and let. In the case
" of a large operation the original lessee who
" deals with the landowner may not himself
" build, but may, after forming the roads and
" sewers, agree to sub let portions at higher
" rents than he himself is paying, and in this
" way there may be one or more intermediaries

"between the landowner and the actual builder.
"The profits of these intermediaries consist in
"the excess during the term which the leases
"have to run of the rents which they are
"entitled to receive over the rents which they
"have to pay, and it seems that they may realise
"their profits in at least the three following
"ways, viz. :—(1) By selling this difference of
"rental to the general public, in which case the
"property sold is obviously a terminable annuity,
"having the same number of years to run as the
"leases, and is sometimes therefore spoken of
"as an improved *leasehold* ground-rent ; or
"(2) by selling the difference of rental to the
"landowner, in which case this difference is
"added to and increases the freehold ground-
"rent which he was otherwise entitled to receive ;
"or (3) by allowing the landowner to take this
"difference of rental as before, in addition to and
"by way of increase of his ground-rent, on the
"terms that the whole of this increased ground-
"rent is to be considered part of the total rent
"payable by the intermediary to the landlord,
"with the result that the intermediary is the
"sooner entitled to leases of the remainder of
"the estate at a nominal rent."

Illustration of 99 years system.

The general terms in which the above account is couched may be rendered plainer by a concrete illustration. Let us assume that A, a landowner, agrees to grant 99 years leases to B, an intermediary, of a building estate of 20 acres at a rent of £25 per acre, or £500 in all ; and that five houses per acre, or one hundred houses in all, are to be built upon the estate. And let us further assume that B, after making the roads and sewers and developing the estate generally, is enabled to let off the estate to the actual builders C, D, E, F....... in small portions and for the residue of the term of 99 years (less one day) at rents which, after allowing for the portions of land occupied by roads, amount to £60 per acre, or £1,200 in all.* On the working out of the contracts by the erection of the houses, and assuming that the ground-rents are evenly distributed over all the houses, B will become entitled to take up 100 separate leases each of one house for 99 years at a ground-rent of £5, and will be bound to grant to C, D, E, F....... 100 separate leases of the same houses for terms of 99 years less one day, and at a rent of £12 for each house. The beneficial interest which B will therefore acquire in return for his expenditure and risk will consist of 100 separate net annual rents of £12 − £5, or £7, lasting for a term of 99 years and no longer. These terminable annuities are currently known as "leasehold ground-rents," or "improved leasehold ground-rents," the word "leasehold" denoting that B's reversionary interest is of a terminable or leasehold character, and the word "improved" denoting that the rents are not derived from the original value of the land, but are due to the improvement in the value of the land which has been caused by the expenditure and superintendence

* B leases for 99 years *less one day* in order to preserve a *reversion* of one day, to which, as explained above, his rent will be *incident*. The increase of rent from £500 to £1,200 may appear large, but so great are the expenses and risks in transactions of this kind that a current rule of thumb in London is, that the margin of profit of the intermediary only begins when he obtains a rent from the actual builders at least double that which he has contracted to pay to the landowner.

of B. The leasehold reversion to which the rent of B (the intermediary) is incident is, as a rule, only a nominal term or reversion of a day or two; but sometimes (as in the case of many of the houses built under the late Mr. Cubitt on the Duke of Westminster's Pimlico estate) the intermediary may persuade builders to take a term of years (such as 85 years) several years shorter than that to which he is himself to become entitled, and in that case he will get his improved rents of £7 for the first 85 years, and the rack-rentals of the houses for the remaining 14 years.

Realisation of profit of development.

It now remains for B, in the instance above stated, to realise the capital value of his improved leasehold ground-rents in order to recoup himself for the capital expenditure incurred; and this he may, according to Mr. Knowles' draft report, effect in any one of at least three ways. He may in the first place sell to a purchaser the improved leasehold ground-rents—that is, the right to receive out of each house a net rent of £7 for a period of 99 years. Or, secondly, he may sell to the landowner for a lump sum the right to let a house direct to the builder, C, at the rent of £12 which C has agreed to pay, instead of letting it to him, B, at a rent of £5. Or, thirdly, while allowing the landowner to let to C direct at £12, he may stipulate that this extra rent shall not be paid for in cash, but shall be taken into account against the total rent of £500 which B has to provide for the landowner; the result being that in case, say, the first forty houses were so let by the landowner, A, to the builders, C, D, and E, at a total ground-rent of £480, the intermediary would be entitled to leases of the sites of the remaining sixty houses (which he has himself agreed to lease to F, G. . . . at rents of £12 each) at an aggregate rental of £20; of which perhaps £1 would be apportioned on each of the first twenty of these houses, while the others would be taken by B at a nominal rent of a peppercorn. And B would thus in this third case, while making no direct profit on the first forty houses built, become entitled to improved leasehold ground-rents of £11 on each of the next twenty houses and of £12 on each of the last forty houses, which he may dispose of in any method he pleases. The practice is in fact very general to secure the total ground-rent payable to the landowner, or the bulk of it, as early as possible on the houses first built; and thus to leave only small or nominal ground-rents on the sites of the houses last built, which are called "remainder-plots," and to which the intermediary looks to secure his profit.

But there is yet another method (not noticed in the passage cited from Mr. Knowles' draft report) in which B may realise his leasehold ground-rents. Instead of disposing of them to the landowner in augmentation of the rents to which he would otherwise be entitled, he may sell them to the builders, C, D, E, F, in reduction of the rents which they would otherwise have to pay, thus entitling them to take up leases from the landowner at the £5 ground-rent at which he had agreed to let to B, instead of at the £12 ground-rent at which B had agreed to let to C, D, E, F. And if this process takes place with regard to a "remainder-plot" to a lease of which B has become entitled at a rent of £1 or at a nominal rent, B can sell to the builder the right to take up his

Additional method of realisation.

lease at this still lower or even nominal rent, instead of at the rent of £5 or £12.*

Existing ground-rents do not represent real rent.

And there is at least one other way in which the ground-rents actually reserved on building-leases are very far from representing the actual rent for the site. It frequently happens that the rental value of the houses when built would be sufficient to adequately secure larger ground-rents than have been agreed to be reserved on the leases under which they are to be held; and in such cases it is not unusual, either under a clause in the building agreement or under arrangements subsequently made, for the builder to "improve" his ground-rent—that is, to accept leases

* A good practical illustration of this method was given by Mr. Ryde in his evidence before the Select Committee on Town Holdings (1886), 8,021 *et seq.* It appears that the late Mr. Cubitt, who had taken a very large tract of land in Pimlico on building agreement from the late Marquis of Westminster, had, by the time Warwick Square came to be built over, provided the total ground-rent payable to the Marquis, and was entitled to take up leases of the Warwick Square houses at a nominal ground-rent of 1s. per annum each. Mr. Cubitt did not himself build the Warwick Square houses, but made sub-agreements with other builders for this purpose, these builders agreeing to take up leases from Mr. Cubitt at a ground-rent of £1 per foot frontage, or of £26 on a house with a 26-foot frontage. Mr. Ryde built a house for himself on these terms, and was consequently entitled to a lease from Mr. Cubitt at £26 ground-rent. But instead of this he purchased Mr. Cubitt's right to a lease at 1s. a year from the Marquis by paying Mr. Cubitt 25 years' purchase of the difference between 1s. and £26, or a capital sum of £648 15s.; and a lease was thereupon granted to Mr. Ryde direct from the Marquis at 1s. a year.

On the other hand, a neighbour of Mr. Ryde's, who was, like him, entitled to a lease from Mr. Cubitt at £26 ground-rent, did not care to invest his money at 4 per cent. in the purchase of Mr. Cubitt's interest. He therefore took up a lease from Mr. Cubitt at £26, and Mr. Cubitt took up a lease from the Marquis at 1s.; Mr. Cubitt's profit in this case, therefore, being represented, not by a capital sum, but by an annuity during the continuance of the leases of £25 19s. per annum.

from the landowner at higher ground-rents than were agreed on, upon payment by the landowner of a certain number of years' purchase of the excess of the ground-rents actually reserved over those agreed to be reserved.

Such then are some of the complications which, when an estate in or near London is developed on the building-lease or 99 years system, affect the determination of the ground-rents actually reserved under the leases in question. It will be particularly observed that the ground-rents actually reserved on particular houses may *exceed* the ground-rents really agreed to be accepted by the landowner in one or more of the following ways, that is to say: (1) by the apportionment of a disproportionate rent on the houses first built; (2) by the landowner having purchased from the intermediary and merged in his ground-rent the improved leasehold ground-rent which represents the outlay of the intermediary on roads, sewers, and general development; and (3) by the landowner having purchased from the builder and added to the agreed ground-rent an extra or improved rent, which really represents an annuity secured on land in return for a cash payment. And it will also be noticed that the ground-rents actually reserved on other houses may fall short of the ground-rents really agreed to be accepted, and may in fact be merely nominal, because the landowner has already had his total ground-rent secured to him, and the sites of these houses represent " remainder-plots." But as to all these elements of calculation which have in fact determined the ground-rents actually reserved the leases themselves are absolutely silent. There is nothing in the leases to show why

Causes which affect amounts of ground-rents.

two exactly similar adjoining houses are leased in the one case at a ground-rent of £25 and in the other case at a ground-rent of a peppercorn. And it would be as hopeless in all these cases to attempt to discover for practical purposes what the unimproved ground was really let for by the landowner as it would be in cases where the landowner has himself made the roads and sewers, and developed the property generally, to try to ascertain how much of the ground-rent at which he afterwards lets the land is the result of natural value, and how much is due to the expenditure which he has incurred.

Existing ground-rents are no measure even of the former, far less of the present value of the houses out of which they are reserved.

CHAPTER II.

THE DETERMINATION OF GROUND-RENT.

IN the previous chapter some examination has been made of the most prevalent systems of developing building land and of paying the landowner the consideration or price for his land. It now becomes necessary to inquire what are the circumstances which determine the amount of that consideration or price, whether it be taken in the shape of a lump sum or of an annual rent-charge or of a ground-rent reserved on a lease for 999 or 99 years or any other period. It is fairly obvious, and is completely borne out by the evidence which has been given before the Select Committee on Town Holdings, that, as between the various systems themselves, the landowner will get the best return for his land by choosing that system which is the most popular in the particular district in which the land is situate; and that the greater interest given to the builder under a grant in fee subject to a rent-charge, or for a term of 999 years, will be compensated for by the rent-charges or rents under that system being, *cæteris paribus*, slightly higher than the rents under the 99 years system. But it is equally clear that there must be many general causes which will affect the value of, or the amount of the consideration to be paid for, land quite independently of the particular mode in which that consideration has to be liquidated.

How is the price or rent of building land fixed?

The same circumstances which will cause an increase in the price paid for land in case it is bought for a lump sum will, as a rule, cause an equally large increase in the ground-rent which would be offered for a 99 years lease of the same piece of land, should it be advisable to develop it by that process. An increase or diminution in demand will cause a simultaneous and equivalent rise or fall both in prices and in rents. It is the object of this chapter to consider how the amount of the price or rent paid for building land is in fact determined.

<small>Monopoly hardly exists and is not considered.</small> And here it should be premised that the case considered is the ordinary one in which there is no monopoly, or no extortion due to monopoly, on either side. It is supposed that the landowner, though naturally anxious to obtain the best price or rent for his land, is willing to let it for building purposes and is not inclined to drive intending builders to other neighbourhoods, and that there are several builders able and willing to commence building operations upon remunerative terms. That this assumption is in fact a true one seems to have been established by the evidence before the Select Committee as to the extreme competition which prevails, not only between different owners in the same district, but between different districts, and by the <small>p. 21.</small> following very moderately worded passage from the Report of the Select Committee:—

> " As regards the first objection " (namely, that the landlord is enabled to obtain an unfair advantage over his tenants by charging an excessive ground-rent on granting the lease), " the Com-
> " mittee think that the builder who, in the vast

"majority of cases, is the person who takes the
"land on which houses are built, is competent
"to make his own bargain with the landowner,
"and that in most instances the original lessee
"probably makes a good profit out of the
"transaction. Some illustrative cases are given
"by Mr. Bourne and Mr. Spain of the large
"profits made by builders and lessees. Another
"check on excessive ground-rents is the frequent
"competition between building estates; so that,
"if a landowner asks too high a rent, he drives
"building away from his own to other pro-
"perties. It is impossible for the Committee
"to give a general opinion on the question of
"how far ground-rents are reasonable in amount.
"This question must be left to be settled
"between the contracting parties, and the Com-
"mittee have no evidence before them that
"when the freehold is sold for building purposes
"the conditions are usually more moderate, or
"that the grievance in question is one specially
"connected with the leasehold system."

And it may also be well to state explicitly an assumption which has been impliedly made in the previous account of the English building systems, namely, that the person who builds is not as a rule an individual building, either by himself or through contractors, for his own occupation, nor even an investor building in order to keep and let the houses for the purposes of investment, but a professional or speculative builder who makes a business of building houses for the purpose of afterwards disposing of them at a profit. The considerations that determine the

Building is done by the professional builder.

price or rent to be paid for building land might probably be shown to be the same in both of the first above-mentioned cases as in the last. But the question is to some extent simplified by considering the operations of the speculative builder; and that it is he who provides the great bulk of the houses of the community is stated in the passage last cited from the Report of the Committee, and there is (apart from common knowledge) ample evidence to prove.

<small>Vigers (1887), 1,078. Tewson (1887), 2,963. Ryde (1886), 7,850 et seq.</small>

Now, a very little consideration will show that the primary object of the speculative builder is to *sell* his houses, not to let them. No doubt, if he is unable to sell, he will often let his houses for a while, in order to keep down the interest on his mortgages and any rent-charge or rent which he may have to pay, and partly also because he can sell better *for investment* when the houses are let than when they are empty. But until the houses are sold, whether they are let or unlet, a certain portion of the builder's capital is locked up in them, and he must always be trying to liberate his capital by a sale in order to subsequently apply it in the further development of his business. As was well said by the Eastbourne agent of the Duke of Devonshire, these builders build to "sell and build again." It follows therefore that the success or failure of the speculative builder will depend on the *price* which he is able to obtain for his houses, and that it is to this that he must look in all his calculations. What, then, is it which determines the price which will be given for a house?

<small>The builder builds to sell.</small>

<small>Wallis (1888), 2,771.</small>

The answer to this last question is not far to seek. All investors are aware that the price of any property is the product of two factors, namely, first, the amount of income derived from the property, and

<small>Price determined by income and security.</small>

secondly, the number of years' purchase which that ncome is worth This latter factor depends upon a number of general considerations, such as the stability of the investment, the fixity or variability of the income, the trouble and expense caused in the collection of the income and the supervision of the property, the comparative ease or difficulty which will be met with in realising the investment, and the prospect of future increase or decrease in its capital or income value. And it is obviously not in the builder's power to control this factor, or any one of the elements in it, except by agreeing (as we already suppose him to have done) to acquire such an interest in the land and house as is in accordance with the custom of the neighbourhood and therefore forms a well-understood and marketable commodity. Supposing, to take a definite instance, that a builder, in order to recoup all his building expenses (using the term in the widest possible sense) and to obtain an ordinary trade profit, must obtain a price of £1,360 for a house of a certain quality, and that houses of this quality are worth 17 years' purchase of the net income derived from them if held * (a) subject to a freehold rent-charge or (b) on a 999 years lease at a ground-rent, and are only worth 16 years' purchase of the same net income if held (c) on a 99 years lease at a ground-rent, it is obvious that his saleable interest in the house provided by him must produce in cases (a) and (b) a net rental of £1,360÷17, or £80 per annum, and in case (c) a net rental of £1,360÷16, or £85 per annum. How, then, is the builder to ensure that his interest in the house shall produce the net rental required?

Builder must look to the net rental he can sell.

* The case of the determination of the capital price of building land under the freehold-purchase system is separately stated later.

The ground-rent is the only elastic element in determining net rental.

The net rental which the builder can dispose of to a purchaser will clearly be the net rack-rental obtained or obtainable from the house, after deducting the rent-charge or ground-rent which the builder has agreed to pay. And here, again, one of these two amounts, namely, the rack-rental, cannot be *controlled* by the builder, but can only be *estimated* by him. But having once made this estimate, he can profitably afford to offer as a rent-charge or a ground-rent for the site of the house the whole excess of the estimated clear rack-rental value over the fixed net rental which he has to provide for his purchaser. Assuming that, in the case supposed, the house which the builder can build to sell for £1,360 will let to a tenant at a clear rack-rental of £100, the builder will be able to offer £100−£80, or £20, as a rent-charge for the fee simple of the site or a ground-rent for a 999 years lease of it, and will be able to offer £100−£85, or £15, as a ground-rent on a 99 years lease. Assuming, again, that through over-building, depression of trade, or any one of a thousand causes, the demand for houses in the neighbourhood slackens, and houses of the cost and quality in question fetch a clear rack-rental of only £95, the builder will on all *future* * contracts be able to offer only £95−£80, or £15, as a rent-charge for the fee simple of the site or a ground-rent on a term of 999 years, and only £95−£85, or £10, as a ground-rent on a 99 years lease. Assuming, lastly, that through increased facilities of access, a change of fashion, or any other of the equally numerous causes which may

---

* With regard to existing agreements, the loss or benefit will in the cases supposed be the builder's. He has then *pro tanto* assumed the position and risks of the landowner.

increase the competition for houses in a locality, the clear rack-rental value of the houses in question can be fairly estimated at £110, the builder will in all future agreements be able to secure his ordinary trade profit after offering £110−£80, or £30, as a rent-charge in perpetuity or a ground-rent on a 999 years lease, or £110−£85, or £25, as a ground-rent on a lease for 99 years. *Any increase or decrease in the prospective rack-rentals of the property must tend to fall exclusively on the annual payments to be offered for the hire of the ground, since these annual payments form the only elastic and modifiable element in the contract.*

The same proposition may easily be shown to be true when the consideration for the land takes the form of a lump sum. At 17 years' purchase the house in question will be worth £1,615 if it can be let for £95 per annum, £1,700 if it can be let for £100 per annum, and £1,870 if it can be let for £110 per annum. But in every one of these cases the cost to the builder will be precisely the same, namely, £1,360. And he will therefore be able to offer to the landowner a price of £1,615−£1,360, or £255, of £1,700−£1,360, or £340, and of £1,870−£1,360, or £510, as the case may be. Here too the price to be paid for the land is the only modifiable, and therefore the only variable, term in the contract. So is the price for the land, if sold.

The vital point, therefore, for the landowner is the amount of the rack-rent which tenants of the houses to be erected on his land may be expected to pay. The landowner will tend to gain or lose in the price or annual payment to be made for his land to the full extent of any increase or decrease in the estimated amounts of these rack-rents. The probable rack-rent is *the* thing.

A few paragraphs may here be devoted to meeting by anticipation two objections that may perhaps be This is so in practice.

urged to the conclusion that has been just arrived at. It will be said, for instance, that many or most builders do not, when tendering for an area of building land, go into any such elaborate calculation as the foregoing of the exact cost of their house, the exact net income they must provide for prospective purchasers, and the exact rack-rental which they will be able to obtain from future tenants. This may be quite true in individual cases, and yet a calculation on this basis may still have been made indirectly and roughly instead of directly and accurately. In all businesses there are certain rules of thumb based on the calculations and experience of other persons or other transactions, which enable individuals to arrive at fairly correct conclusions without any immediate reference to the premises on which those conclusions are based. A builder has himself experienced, or has learnt from the experience of others, that in a particular neighbourhood, or in neighbourhoods that offer about the same residential advantages, a certain price or rental has been given for building land, with a view to the erection of a particular class of houses, and that the bargain has resulted in a profit either equal to, exceeding, or falling short of the usual profit, or perhaps has even resulted in a loss. The profit or loss that has occurred is in fact the result of the causes which have been examined above. But the builder can in making any new bargain avoid considering directly the operation of these causes, and can make an offer based roughly, but with sufficient accuracy for his purpose, on the *results* of the previous transactions.

Again, it is sometimes said that any increase or decrease in the rack-rents which may be expected from the houses to be built in a neighbourhood will not affect the landowner to the *whole* extent of the change, but will be partly shared by the builders with whom he deals.* No doubt there is always some delay in complete adjustment to any change. And during the interval other persons may share in a profit or a loss than those who will ultimately have to receive or bear the whole of it. In such cases the estimates of value have not during the interval followed to its full extent the change in actual value. But subject to this qualification there seems to be no reason for thinking that any part of a change of value *ultimately* affects anyone but the landowner. There is no reason why the average profit of a builder who contracts to cover a site in the City worth £1,000,000 per acre should exceed that of a builder who contracts to cover land lying on the utmost outskirts of a town and worth from £100 to £150 per acre.

The whole loss or gain is in fact the landowner's.

One further point remains to be noticed with regard to the determination of the price or annual payment to be made for building land, and that is whether there is any minimum which it must equal or exceed before the land is devoted to building purposes, and how that minimum is ascertained. It appears to me that there is such a minimum, and that it is ascertained with reference to the value of land for agricultural or other productive purposes. It is indeed often said that, although this may be so theoretically, it is not so in practice, because the rent

Minimum ground-rents.

---

* Here again it is only future agreements that are spoken of. As to existing agreements the builder will alone get any profit or bear any loss, unless indeed in the latter case he fails and the landowner has to make a fresh agreement with another builder at a lower rent.

for building purposes is so much higher than for agricultural purposes. But those who maintain this seem to lose sight of several material circumstances which it may be worth while to set out.

<small>There is a real competition between land for accommodation and building purposes.</small>

On the one hand the rent of land near a town for agricultural or productive purposes is very much higher than any ordinary agricultural rent. "Accommodation" land, such as this land is called, will often fetch £5 or £6 per acre for the feed of horses and cattle; and even higher rents are often obtained for the use of such land as cricket or football grounds, racing or coursing grounds, or for the hundred and one other purposes to which land in the neighbourhood of a considerable community may be turned. And on the other hand there are many risks and great expenses involved in actually rendering building land available as such. It has been seen that roads and sewers must directly or indirectly be constructed by the landowner; and the cost of these, which is always heavy, naturally eats up a far larger proportion of the ultimate rent or price where the value of land is low. Then again, in new neighbourhoods there are far greater risks of deterioration through a change of fashion, the construction of some new means of communication to a competing locality, or some other equally potent cause, than in old and well settled districts. Once more, it has always to be remembered that an owner developing his land for building purposes parts with it, and with all possibility of future increment in it, either for ever, or at any rate for a very long period, equivalent even under the 99 years system to three generations; and that therefore the price or rent asked for land to be devoted to building purposes must, to tempt a landowner, substantially exceed the rent which he can obtain for the land for short periods while still retaining its future increment for himself. And lastly, one seems almost able to place one's finger on land which is in fact let or sold for building purposes, or (if the phrase may be allowed) for semi-building purposes, at a rent scarcely exceeding that of accommodation land, as one notices the comparatively large areas of ground surrounding the villas which cluster round the railway stations from fifteen to thirty miles from London.

For all these reasons, though I cannot claim to have any special knowledge on the subject, it seems to me that in practice as well as in theory the value of land for agricultural purposes does in fact form a minimum determining (after the allowances I have mentioned) the lowest price or rent that will be taken for land for building purposes; and that the experience of surveyors and other persons accustomed to deal with land in districts just beginning to acquire value for building would be that there is a real, and not merely a theoretical, competition for the use of land between agriculture and bricks and mortar. And it will also be noticed that land on the outskirts of building, which would command a tangible price or annual payment either on a grant in fee or on a lease for 999 years, may not be able to bear any rent at all on a lease for so comparatively short a period as 99 years.

Josiah Thomas (1888), 3134-5.

CHAPTER III.

HAVE GROUND-RENTS ALREADY PAID RATES?

Are ground-rents affected by rates? So far, the conclusion has been arrived at that the price that will be given, or the annual payment that will be made, for a piece of building land is dependent on the price that will be given, or the clear rack-rental that will be paid, for the land and house together, when the latter has been built; or, to put the proposition in a form which is almost self-evident, that the value of a piece of building land is the estimated value of the land when covered, less the cost (including delay, risk, profit, and every kind of expense) of covering it; and that the rent that will be given for a piece of building land is the estimated rack-rental of the land when covered, less such a rent as will under the conditions of the holding be an equivalent for the cost (inclusive as before) of covering the land. It is still necessary to inquire how the rack-rental of the house and land together is determined, and in particular whether this rack-rental is in any way lessened or affected by the rates which are paid by the occupier at a rack-rent. For any decrease in the rack-rent which may be due to this cause will, as well as that due to any other cause, be thrown exclusively on the only available margin, namely, the price to be given for the land or the rent-charge or ground-rent to be paid for it. To avoid cumbrousness of expression, the alternatives of "price" and "rent-charge" (which clearly depend on the same principles) will be left out of account, and the case of a ground-rent only will be considered.

Ever since Ricardo's celebrated exposition, his theory of rent has been substantially adopted by all the leading writers on political economy. A statement of the theory in its application to the rents of houses may be taken from the essay * to which reference has already been made in the preface:— <small>Ricardo's theory of rent.</small>

"The theory is generally stated with regard
"to agricultural land, that being the kind of
"land of the greatest importance to the political
"economist. It is assumed (though the truth
"of the assumption is not vital to the theory)
"that there is in any one stage of society land
"just on the margin of cultivation—that is, land
"which can just be cultivated so as to yield
"average interest and profit on the capital em-
"ployed if no rent is paid for it. It is then
"asserted that the rent paid for any superior
"land is the measure of the superiority for pro-
"duction which this land possesses over the
"land just on the margin of cultivation. And
"the consequence follows that, as the necessities
"of increasing population compel resort to the
"cultivation of soil inferior to the least produc-
"tive soil previously cultivated, the rents of all
"lands previously cultivated must rise, inasmuch
"as their superiority is increased when tested
"with reference to a lowered standard.

"Now, precisely the same line of reasoning

* Ground-rents and Building-Leases, pp. 132 to 135.

" is applicable to the occupation-rents of houses.
" There are, of course, many sites in the king-
" dom where it would not pay to build a house
" rent free. That is, an occupation-rent could
" not be obtained for the house sufficient to
" afford ordinary interest on the sum expended
" in its construction; or, in other words, the
" occupation-rent would be so low that a pur-
" chaser buying on this rent would give a price
" less than the sum that had been expended in
" the construction of the buildings. But in the
" infinite and continuous gradations of suit-
" ability in sites for the erection of houses,
" there are many sites to be found where it
" would just pay, and no more than pay, to
" erect a house rent free. That is, the occupa-
" tion-rent which would there be obtained for a
" house would be just sufficient, and no more
" than sufficient, to yield an ordinary profit on
" the cost of construction, or, in other words,
" to induce a purchaser to purchase at the actual
" cost of construction.

" Such land as has just been mentioned may
" be said to lie on the building limit. And the
" Ricardian theory may be said to be more
" obviously true with regard to houses than with
" regard to agricultural land. For while it is
" difficult to point out agricultural land actually
" let without rent, it is easy enough to point
" out houses, or even whole neighbourhoods of
" houses, which from various causes are now
" let at a rent only sufficient, or even less than
" sufficient, to yield ordinary profit on their
" mere cost of construction.

"Now, assuming that a house just on the building limit is let at a rack-rent of £50, the rack-rent of a similar house in a more favourite district will exceed this sum of £50 by an amount which measures the superiority for residential or business purposes, in the eye of an occupier, of the second position over the first. Now, as population increases, and the less and less favoured sites are built over, the difference for residential purposes between the sites on the building limit and the picked sites, which have long since been built over, becomes more and more marked. And as the rent for the house on the picked site exceeds that for the house on the building margin in proportion to this superiority, while there is no reason for supposing that the rent of the house on the building limit (that is, the rent for the mere buildings) will at all decrease, the consequence is that the rents for houses on the picked sites must, on the whole, tend continually to increase."

The rack-rent of every house will, therefore, be the aggregate of two elements, namely, first, the rent representing the cost of the structure, and secondly, the rent measuring the superiority of the residential advantages of that house over houses on the building limit, which is, in fact, the rental value of the site.* Near the outskirts for the

The elements of rack-rent.

* The same conclusion as in the last chapter is thus arrived at by a somewhat different and shorter process, namely, that the ground-rent is the estimated clear rack-rent less the rent representing the cost of building.

time being of a town the first element will form the larger part of the rack-rental; in the more central parts the latter element will become more and more important in proportion to the advantages of the position. It will be found that this separation of rack-rental into its two elements, though sufficiently obvious in itself, is of great importance in considering the incidence of rates.

At first all rates seem to fall on ground-rents.

The first and most obvious view with regard to the effect of rates on rack-rents is that the rates will to their full extent be deducted from, and operate to diminish, the rack-rents which would be otherwise paid. And this view would seem to be borne out by the generally accepted axiom of political economy that a tax on land in proportion to its rental value, on whomsoever levied, must fall wholly on the rent. For the rent is a payment measuring, in the eye of the occupier, the superiority of the land he occupies over the worst land which it is just profitable to occupy rent free.* But if the occupation of the superior land necessarily involves a payment to the State or local authority in proportion to the amount of that superiority, the payment which the occupier will make to the owner must necessarily be diminished by that amount, since otherwise he would be paying altogether for the superiority of the land he occupies more than it is actually worth. Or, to put what is really the same argument from the rough, practical point of view of everyday experience,

---

* Mill, *Principles of Political Economy*, Book V. chap. iv. § 3 (p. 507, People's Edition, 1865): "A tax proportioned to the rent would fall wholly " on the rent, and would not at all raise the price of corn, which is " regulated by the portion of the produce that pays no rent." *i.e.*, which is produced on land which pays no rent.

the tenant always takes into account the rates and taxes he will have to pay on his houses as part of his rent, and in almost all cases makes particular inquiries on this point before taking his house; and the whole amount of these rates and taxes is therefore thrown on, and deducted by anticipation from, the rent he will agree to pay.

If, then, the whole amount of the rates in a locality is deducted from and operates to decrease the rack-rents which can be obtained in that locality, it is clear from what has prece led that the whole amount of the prospective rates to be levied on the estimated rack-rentals of the houses to be built on an estate will be deducted by anticipation from, and operate in diminution of, the ground-rent which will be offered for that estate by builders. Ground-rents, in fact, will have borne the whole rates not only on the rent for the sites but on the whole rack-rentals of houses and sites together.

This view of the subject has in fact been taken in a document of no less authority than the very able draft Report submitted by Mr. Goschen to the Select Committee on Local Taxation which was nominated by the House of Commons on the 3rd March, 1870. The main subject of the Report is the incidence of local taxation in country districts, which involves distinct considerations from and is no part of the subject of these pages. But the following passage deals briefly and pregnantly with the case of rates on house property:— *This is the view of Mr. Goschen's draft Report.*

"To return to the case of house property,
"it has been stated that the incidence of rates
"must there be considered with reference to

"three parties—the owner of the soil, the
"builder, and the occupier. On making the
"same distinction as in the case of land, between
"the moment when the first bargain is made
"and the subsequent period during which no
"readjustment takes place, it is clear that in the
"former case the owner pays the bulk, if not the
"whole, of the rates. The builder calculates on
"a certain profit, or else he would not build;
"he knows that tenants of a certain class can
"afford to give a certain rent, and no more, for
"a certain kind of house; and, therefore, if
"building is to take place at all, it is clear that
"the rates must fall there where alone a margin
"exists to bear them; that is to say, on the
"price given, or ground-rent promised to the
"owner of the soil."*

And again:

"To sum up the case of house property
"generally, it appears that the owners of building

* The subsequent much longer paragraph—in which it is stated that rates may be so high that builders will not build at any ground-rent that will be accepted, and then the supply of houses will be checked until it again becomes profitable to build—is not quoted, because it depends upon the principle of the passage quoted which is not here accepted in its entirety, and because (in accordance with this principle) it draws no distinction between the rent representing the cost of the building and that representing the superiority of the site. In the case supposed I think that, on the view taken later on, the rates on the building-rent (so far as not "differential") will be thrown mainly on the occupier, but the "differential" rates on the building and the whole rates on any ground-rent will be thrown on the ground-rent. It is of course obvious that the landowner suffers *some* loss through the high rates, since during the cessation of building he is *entirely* deprived of the ground-rent which he would otherwise have received.

"land, like the owners of other land, have to
"submit to a reduction of rent equivalent to the
"average amount of rates which the builder or
"other lessee calculates that he would have to
"pay according to the average of past rates."

This view, that the whole of the rates and taxes on the prospective rack-rents of houses will be thrown by anticipation on the owners of the land which is to form the sites of the houses, is also the practical view of the subject—that is, the opinion held in general by most of the surveyors and land agents who are professionally concerned in the development of building land—and no doubt contains a very considerable element of truth and is confirmed to a certain extent by some of the concrete illustrations which I propose hereafter to give. And in my previous essay on Ground-rents and Building-Leases I adopted this view as the true one, and enforced it to the best of my ability.* But subsequent reflection has brought me to the conclusion that this view is to some extent an over-statement of the amount of the rates and taxes which fall upon building land, and that only a large proportion, and not the whole, of the rates on the ultimate rack-rentals is cast by anticipation on the ground-rents agreed to be paid.

This view, however, is not quite accura'e.

Let us recur to the division of rack-rent which has been previously made, and which is also adopted

---

* I am indebted to Mr. Wm. Mathews, of Birmingham, the well-known surveyor, for pointing out to me that I was in error in making use, for the purposes of the argument there, of Mill's views upon the incidence of taxes on rent generally, without particularly alluding to the special views which he also held as to the incidence of taxes on the rack-rentals of houses. I am glad to think that my present views have the advantage of being in substantial accordance with those of Mr. Mathews.

All rates on the ground-rent fall on it in advance.

by Mill in his investigation of the subject,* into rent for the site and rent for the structure. The rent for the site is, as Mill remarks, determined by the ordinary principles of rent—that is, by the superiority of the site over the least valuable site used for the same purpose. And therefore any tax proportioned to this rent must necessarily be borne by the owner. Assuming, for instance, that the business superiority of a shop fronting on Cheapside over a shop in the Edgware Road is measured by an intending occupier at £500 a year, and that the rates in each district are 5s. in the £, the occupier will clearly not offer £500 more rent in the one case than in the other, since he will also have to pay an additional sum of £125 in rates, and his total extra annual outlay for the more valuable shop would thus be £625, or £125 more than the superiority of position warrants. He will offer only £400 extra rent; and this, with the £100 which will be added to that extra rent in the shape of rates, will be the exact equivalent of the business superiority of the shop in Cheapside.

As regards "building-rent" rates must be divided.

On the other hand, when so much of the rack-rent as is rent for the structure comes to be dealt with, other considerations apply, and it becomes necessary to distinguish between those parts of the rates which are fairly constant throughout the kingdom and which may for this purpose be designated " constant " rates, and those parts of the rates

* *Principles of Political Economy*, Book V. chapter iii. § 6 (p. 501, People's Edition). Mill's ultimate view that the rates on the ground-rent of houses fall on the landowner is of special significance, because this is a correction of the view which he previously entertained and expressed (though under certain limitations which rendered it rather impractical) in the earlier editions of his work, that the rates on this portion of the rack-rental, as well as on the rent for the structure, fell on the occupier.

which are different or variable in different parts of the kingdom and may in like manner be called "differential" rates. The best example of a "constant" rate (though it is not strictly a rate at all) is the inhabited house duty, which is imposed on all inhabited buildings (of a certain value) alike throughout England. And a good example of a variable rate is the School Board rate, which is approaching 1s. in the £ in London and is non-existent in many parts of England. But for the purposes of the present discussion it is probably fairer not to distinguish between the parts of every individual rate that are respectively constant and variable (in which case an overwhelming proportion of the rates on houses would be found to be variable or "differential"), but to distinguish between those parts of the *totals* of the rates which are respectively "constant" and "differential." For it is by the total of the rates and not by the particular items of which the total is composed that the occupier will be affected. If, for instance, 1s. 6d. in the £ may be taken as a not extraordinary minimum total for rates proper in thoroughly rural districts, and 6s. in the £ may be taken as a not extraordinary maximum total for rates in a large town,* the "constant" existing rates will be 1s. 6d. in the £, and the "differential" rates will be 4s. 6d. in the £, without entering into an elaborate examination of the respective amounts of the various rates making up the two totals.

* I am not here professing to take the average rates in country districts or in towns, but rather the lowest rates in the former case and the highest in the latter, that are not so low or so high (as the case may be) as to be absolutely abnormal. And even so it is not minute accuracy but only a rough estimate that is here aimed at.

The "constant" rates on building-rents fall on occupiers,

Now, as regards the "constant" rates, the 1s. 6d. in the £, it appears to me that the occupier, as the consumer of the house, must necessarily bear at any rate the great bulk of them. Go where he will within the boundaries of the kingdom he cannot escape them. Even on the "building limit," where ground-rents are *ex hypothesi* nothing or next to nothing, these rates must still be borne by the rent representing the structure, which is all that is now being considered. Builders are under no obligation to build, and will not do so unless they can obtain a remunerative rent for their buildings in addition to and beyond any rates that may have to be paid. And therefore, as in the case of taxes on other commodities, the production of buildings will cease until the rents offered by occupiers have advanced to a point at which, besides affording a sufficient return for the builder's outlay, they will also cover the rates that have to be provided for.

except to some small amount.

There are, however, at least two causes which tend to throw a part of even the constant rates from the occupier on to the shoulders of the landowner. First, any check on the production of houses due to the increased annual cost to the occupier in consequence of the pressure of the constant rates must necessarily prevent *pro tanto* recourse being had for building purposes to the more unsuitable sites, and so must diminish the superiority of the sites actually used and decrease the rent paid for them. And secondly, the pressure of any burdens such as rates must, in view of the competition which is always going on with foreign countries, tend to some extent to drive or keep the more roving or cosmopolitan class of occupiers out of the country, and to that extent to shift the burden on to rack-rentals. But the aggregate operation of these two causes is probably slight.

On the other hand the whole of the "differential" rates on the rent representing the cost of structure will in my view, by virtue of the competition between lightly and heavily burdened districts, be thrown, not on the occupier, but on the rack-rental and so (as has been already shown) on the only elastic margin, namely, the ground-rent. Assume, for instance, that an occupier is deciding between a house in the country, the whole of the rental of which, say £100, is rent representing the cost of the structure,* and a house in London, the rack-rental of which is £150 per annum, made up of (1) £100 as before for the rent of the structure, and (2) £50 for the rent of the site; and assume also that the rates in the country district in question and in London are respectively 2s. and 5s. in the £. The total outgoings from the country house will then be £100 for rent and £10 for rates on the building-rent; while the total outgoings for the London house will be £150 for rent, £12. 10s. for rates on the rent of the site, and £25 (or an excess of £15) for rates on the building-rent or building value.† And the intending tenant will not occupy the London house in pre-

The "differential" rates on building-rents fall on ground-rents in advance.

---

* This is, in fact, not at all an unusual case. No doubt when a house is first built some rent or price will be charged for the land, but many districts have deteriorated so much that the rents of houses barely represent the cost of building, and new houses would not be erected there if land were given rent free for the purpose.

† The rates will, of course, be levied in a lump on the whole rent of £150, but it is convenient, for the sake of clearness, to separate this rent, and in consequence the rates levied on it, into their component parts. To avoid complexity the fact is not taken into account that the rateable value is less than the rack-rent, but this fact does not affect the argument.

ference to the country house unless the superiority of residential advantages in the former case is measured in his eyes not merely by £50, the excess of rent, but also by £12 10s., the amount of rates on the annual value of the site, and by £15, the excess of rates on the structure, that is, by £77 10s. in all. But we have already seen that the whole superiority of residential advantages of any house, as measured by tenants, does (apart from rates) go in augmentation of the rack-rent of the house. And it is clear, therefore, not merely that the £12 10s., being the amount of the rates on the value of the site, will (as we have already seen in the case of the Cheapside and Edgware Road shops) fall on and be deducted from the rack-rental and therefore by anticipation from the ground-rent of the house in question, but that the same result will also take place with regard to the sum of £15, being the amount of the differential rates at 3s. in the £ on the £100 forming the rent for the structure of the house.

Instances of this in London.

An excellent example of the manner in which "differential" rates are in fact thrown on rack-rentals was given by Mr. (since Sir Henry) Hunt in his evidence before the Select Committee of the House of Commons on Local Taxation, which was appointed in the year 1870. He mentioned that the east side of Lowndes Square was in the parish of St. George, Hanover Square, and the west side was in the parish of St. Luke, Chelsea, and added: " The rates in St. " George, Hanover Square, are comparatively low; " in St. Luke's, Chelsea, they are higher, and *ceteris* " *paribus* a house on the west side would not realise " the same rent as a house on the east side for that " reason." And he also mentioned that for the

773.

same reason a difference existed between the rents of houses in Tachbrook Street, which was also divided between two parishes; and stated subsequently before the same Committee that persons who came to ask his advice as to buying a house always asked what the rates and taxes were, and what they were likely to reach.

4,421.

The true conclusion, then, from the foregoing elaborate investigation appears to be that ground-rents pay the following portions of the rates (so far as they already exist or are reasonably anticipated) on the prospective rack-rentals of the houses that will be erected on the land, namely, (1) the whole rates on so much of the rack-rentals as represents rent for the sites; (2) the "differential" rates (representing about two-thirds or three-quarters of the total rates in highly rated districts) on so much of the rack-rentals as represents rent for the structure; and (3) some unascertainable, but probably small, proportion of the "constant" rates on so much of the rack-rentals as represents rent for the structure: while, on the other hand, the occupiers of the houses, as consumers of the structures, pay the remainder of the rates on the rack-rentals, that is—to put it exactly—the larger proportion of the "constant" rates (representing about one-third or one-quarter of the total rates in highly rated districts) on so much of the rack-rentals as represents rent for the structure. And this conclusion is in substantial accordance with the views of one of the most competent, and perhaps the most careful, of all living English writers on political economy,* as expressed in the following passage:—

Conclusion as to incidence of rates.

* Mr. Henry Sidgwick. *The Principles of Political Economy*, p. 571. Mr. Sidgwick is in substance a follower of Mill, though he

Mr. Henry Sidgwick's view.

"Suppose that a new tax proportional to value—not balanced by corresponding taxes on other sources of income—is laid on owners of land generally, including owners of land with buildings on it; and suppose for simplicity that the tax is annual and rent is competitively determined afresh from year to year. Then, as the imposition of the tax cannot at once affect the supply of houses or the demand for them, the whole tax will at first tend to be paid by the owner; so that the building of houses will become less remunerative, and will consequently be reduced in extent. The resulting limitation of supply —as houses cannot profitably be imported— will tend to raise their price and rent sufficiently to make building remunerative; that is, if the cost of building were unaltered the rent would tend to be increased by the amount of the proportion of the tax that falls on the rent of the building as distinct from the ground. But in fact, if the tax be a heavy one, the rise will tend to be temporarily somewhat less than this; since the cost of building will undergo some reduction in consequence of the check given to the building industry by the tax, which will tend to diminish for a time the returns to the labour and capital employed

suggests corrections of particular doctrines and of many details. For instance, Mill does not draw any distinction between " constant " rates and " differential " rates (speaking, indeed, of a house-*tax*, which was probably regarded by him as " constant "), while Mr. Sidgwick rightly takes the distinction. Mr. Sidgwick, however, does not attempt any estimate of the relative amounts of the " constant " and " differential " rates.

" in this industry. Ultimately, however, the
" whole portion of the tax that is paid for the
" value of the house itself will fall—in the case of
" private dwelling houses—on the consumer or
" occupier. The portion, however, that falls
" on the ground-rent will continue to be borne
" by the owner of the ground (supposing, as
" above explained, that he has not sold it)
" unless the tax has caused a rise in agricultural
" produce,* and the land is so situated that it
" could be as remuneratively employed for
" agricultural purposes as for building. Nay
" further, if the tax be not uniform but higher
" in some districts than in others, the whole
" excess—and not merely the proportion of the
" excess that falls on the ground-rent — will
" tend to remain on the owner ; at least so long
" as the fall does not render the land more
" profitable for other purposes than it is for
" building."

And finally, let the question be tested by the light of common everyday experience, a rough but trustworthy guide in these matters. It is within almost everyone's ordinary observation and knowledge that high rates in any district act as a most distinct discouragement to, and check on, building. It is familiar ground that just outside the boundaries of heavily rated urban or suburban districts buildings are more readily erected than inside those boundaries, just as in Continental towns the *octroi* invites the development of suburban communities immediately outside

Confirmation of this view by common experience.

---

* This possibility appears to be rather remote, and the result would in any case probably be insignificant.

the limits within which the tax in question is imposed. And in the expensive conflicts that sometimes occur on proposals to extend municipal boundaries, and therefore to widen the area of municipal taxation, it is not merely the owners and occupiers of existing houses but the owners of building land within the debateable area who are interested and who unite in opposing the schemes. But the whole argument is conclusively clenched by an example which was given (*alio intuitu*) by a witness before the Select Committee on Town Holdings.

<small>Conclusive instance from Falmouth.</small> Mr. Mackenzie, a witness decidedly in favour both of leasehold enfranchisement and of the direct rating of ground-rents, complained that in certain parts of Falmouth comprising the former possessions of the Killigrew family and now chiefly belonging to Lord Kimberley, there is a special Church-rate of 1s. 4d. in the £ levied by an Act of Charles II. on the possessors of house property; and that in cases where portions of the land affected by the Act have been leased the burden of the rate has been thrown on the lessees. The consequence has been (to quote <small>(1833), 9,798.</small> his own words) that, " to escape that, the builders get " out of the property of Lord Kimberley and go into " Mr. Basset's property at the northern end of the <small>9,804.</small> " town." And again: " That of course is one of the " hindrances to town buildings there for the poorer " class and the working class. *They are obliged to get* " *out of the range of this rate to save the* 1s. 4d. *in* " *the £.*"

<small>Examination of this instance.</small> It is a curious instance of the effect of a *parti pris* that the witness should have regarded the rate levied by this Act as being a hardship and burden primarily

on the builders of houses, and secondarily on the working classes in Falmouth, and should have omitted altogether to notice on whose shoulders the real stress fell. As to the local builders who actually built on parts of the land, they would no doubt have had full cognisance of the existence of the rate and would have protected themselves by offering a lower rent for the land; and so there seems to be no grievance at all in their case. And as to the working classes of Falmouth, they, in common with the rest of that community, would be inconvenienced by not being able to resort to and dwell on the land most available for purposes of residence; but that is the extent of the hardship to them. The persons chiefly injured are, without doubt, the owners of the land, since the effect of this differential rate has been to prevent a great part of their land from being built on at all—in fact, to swallow up the whole of the ground-rental value. It is quite clear that the rate is not merely deducted on so much of the rack-rent of prospective houses as would represent rent for the site; for, taking the rent of a site independently of the tax at £3, this would only reduce the ground-rent offered by 4s.—that is, to £2. 16s.—not eat it up altogether, as is actually the case. The differential rate on the whole rack-rent is clearly deducted by any tenant from the rack-rent he will offer (and therefore, as we have seen, is deducted from the ground-rent); for there is no need for any tenant to pay £50 for a house and (in addition to all ordinary rates) a further rate of 1s. 1d. in the £ on this £50, when he can get a similar house on competing estates for £50 and ordinary rates only; while if the builder pays the rate he cannot for that reason get a higher rent from his tenant than on competing estates, and must compensate himself in advance by offering a ground rent smaller in proportion to the payment. The "differential" Church-rate of 1s. 4d. in the £ on the rack-rent of a house on this estate, amounting in the case supposed to £3. 6s. 8d., must necessarily be wholly thrown on the ground-rent to be offered by the builder, and would in the case supposed (as it has done to a great extent in fact) eat up the ground-rent altogether and cause the ground to lie vacant and idle.

It would be difficult to suggest a more striking illustration of how certainly and automatically differential rates on houses are thrown on the value of the sites on which the houses are to be erected.

CHAPTER IV.

THE PROPOSALS TO RATE GROUND-RENTS.

IN the preceding chapters an attempt has been made to analyse and explain the different methods of payment for building land which are in practical operation in this country; to fix the causes which determine the amounts of those payments, particularly in the case of annual payments or rents; and finally to ascertain how far the rates, which it is estimated will be paid by the occupier, are, in fact, thrown by anticipation on and deducted from a particular kind of annual payment called groundrent. It has been laboriously but, it is hoped, conclusively demonstrated, first, that the price or annual payment that is offered for a building site is dependent on the estimated rack-rental of the site when covered, and that any increase or decrease in the estimate of that rack-rental will involve a corresponding and equal increase or decrease in the price or annual rental offered for the vacant site; and secondly, that there are thrown on a ground-rent by anticipation not only the whole rates on so much of the prospective rack-rental as represents the groundrent itself, but also a considerable portion, and in highly rated urban districts much the larger portion, of the rates on the remainder of the rack-rental. It is clear that the considerations which have established this second proposition with regard to ground-rents

Summary of preceding chapter.

are equally applicable to the incidence of prospective rates on any other form of annual or capital payment for building land. And it may, therefore, be laid down as a fundamental axiom that the owner of an urban building estate, whatever method he applies to its development, pays indirectly, but not the less surely, a large proportion of the estimated rates on the houses to be built there.

<small>Need for stating the proposals actually made.</small>

Having proceeded thus far, it may now be well to inquire what are the proposals which have from time to time, and particularly of late years, been made for effecting some change in the law which at present throws the immediate duty of paying rates on the occupiers of houses above a certain rental value, and does not in general empower them to deduct any part of this rate from the rent they pay their landlords. Not only are these the proposals that have to be dealt with by practical statesmen, and accepted or rejected as the public interest may dictate. But even to the theorist the investigation of definite proposals of any kind is often of invaluable aid, as supplying a practical test of which he is often in need, and compelling him successively either to justify or to abandon every part of his theories, and particularly those parts which involve, or appear to involve, any anomaly or hardship.

<small>The Select Committee of 1866.</small>

In the year 1866 a Select Committee of the House of Commons was appointed to inquire into the Local Government and Local Taxation of the Metropolis; and the Report of this Committee contained a recommendation that, in view of the novelty and magnitude of the works undertaken by the Metropolitan Board, " a portion of the charge for permanent improvements " and works should be borne by the owners of pro- " perty within the Metropolis, the rate being in the

" first instance paid by the occupier, and subsequently
" deducted from his rent, as is now provided in regard
" to the general property tax." The Report, however,
did not deal with any question of setting aside contracts
in cases where the occupier had (as under the usual
building-lease form) covenanted to pay "all rates,
" taxes, and impositions . . . whether charged on
" owners or occupiers." And it is obvious that the
charge on owners of rates for permanent improvements would necessarily involve a rather difficult
distinction being drawn between those rates which
were and those which were not for permanent
improvements, and also (to be quite fair) an elaborate
inquiry being made in every case as to the extent
of the ownership of each owner, and the amount to
which he would therefore benefit by the making of
the permanent improvements. But the recommendation of this Committee and the arguments for and
against it will be more fully considered in the subsequent part of this work, which deals with the
proposal to tax reversions.

The Select Committee on Local Taxation appointed
by the House of Commons in the year 1870, and to
which reference has already been made, were not able
to agree to accept either of the draft reports placed
before them by Mr. Goschen and Mr. Corrance respectively, but ultimately passed certain resolutions
on the subject. As regards urban property these
conclusions lose some of their force, because not
only does the inquiry seem to have been mainly
directed towards agricultural land, but in the resolutions themselves no distinction seems to have been
drawn between the two classes of property. The
more material parts of these resolutions for the present purpose are as follows:—

*The Select Commit-
tee of 1870.*

"1. That your Committee, without pledging
" themselves to the view that all rates should be
" dealt with in the same manner, are of opinion :

" (*a*) That the existing system of local taxation,
" under which the exclusive charge of almost
" all rates leviable upon rateable property for
" current expenditure as well as for new
" objects and permanent works is placed by
" law upon the occupiers, while the owners are
" generally exempt from any direct or imme-
" diate contributions in respect of such rates,
" is contrary to sound policy.
" (*b*) That the evidence taken before your Com-
" mittee shows that in many cases the burden
" of the rates, which are directly paid by the
" occupier, falls ultimately, either in part or
" wholly, upon the owner, who, nevertheless,
" has no share in their administration.
" (*c*) That in any reform in the existing system
" of local taxation it is expedient to adjust the
" system of rating in such a manner that both
" owners and occupiers may be brought to feel
" an immediate interest in the increase or
" decrease of local expenditure, and in the
" administration of local affairs.
" (*d*) That it is expedient to make owners as well
" as occupiers directly liable for a certain
" proportion of the rates.
" (*e*) That, subject to equitable arrangements as
" regards existing contracts, the rates should
" be collected, as at present, from the occupier
" (except in the case of small tenements, for
" which the landlord can now by law be rated),

" power being given to the occupier to deduct
" from his rent the proportion of the rates to
" which the owner may be made liable, and
" provision being made to render persons
" having superior or intermediate interests
" liable to proportionate deductions from the
" rents received by them, as in the case of the
" income tax, with a like prohibition against
" agreements in contravention of the law.

" 3. That in the event of any division of rates
" between the owner and occupier, it is essential
" that such alterations should be made in the
" constitution of the bodies administering the
" rates as would secure a direct representation of
" the owners adequate to the immediate interest
" in local expenditure which they would thus
" have acquired.

" 7. That whilst it is necessary to make pro-
" vision for limiting, as far as practicable, the dis-
" turbance of existing contracts, it would be, on
" many grounds, undesirable, and almost imprac-
" ticable, to extend the exemption of property
" held under leases from the operation of the pro-
" posed changes until the expiration of such leases.

" 9. That the difficulties of the case would
" be equitably met by exempting the owners of
" property held under lease from the proposed
" division of rates for a period of three years, and
" by providing that after the expiration of that
" time the occupiers of such property should be
" entitled, equally with all other occupiers, to
" deduct from the rent the proportionate part of
" the rates to which the owner may become liable,
" power being given to the owner at the same
" time to add to his rent a sum equivalent to the

"like proportionate part of the rates, calculated on the average annual amount of the rates paid by the occupier during the three years above referred to." *

The Select Committee of 1886. In March 1886 a Select Committee of the House of Commons on Town Holdings was, as has been mentioned already, appointed to "inquire into the terms of occupation and the compensation for improvements possessed by the occupiers of town houses and holdings in Great Britain and Ireland"; and there was referred to this Committee later in the same month "the question of imposing a direct assessment on the owners of ground-rents and on the owners of increased values imparted to land by building operations or other improvements." The terms of the latter reference to the Committee indicate the nature of the change demanded by those on whose initiative the reference was made, but no report has yet been made by the Committee on this branch of the inquiry before them. Those witnesses who have hitherto given evidence before the Committee in favour of a change have as a rule demanded in general terms that the whole or some part of local taxation shall be thrown on the landowners in relief of the occupiers, and that with regard both to existing contracts (which are to this extent to be set aside) and to future contracts; and have justified this demand on three main grounds,

---

* It is necessary to set out these proposals as to existing contracts at full length, because all notice of them is often omitted in treatises on the subject. For instance, in the part of the pamphlet by Mr. Moulton mentioned later on, which deals with the question whether landowners have had warning of the proposed changes, he states that this Committee "reported in favour of the occupier being 'entitled to deduct a portion of his rates from his rent," without any mention of the "equitable arrangements as regards existing contracts."

namely, (1) that landlords at present escape local taxation, (2) that they nevertheless are benefited by the expenditure of the rates not only in public improvements but in many other ways, and (3) that even where under existing leases lessees have covenanted to pay the rates there has been an increase of rates that could not have been foreseen. And a change has been demanded not merely by witnesses from places where the London leasehold system prevails, but by a witness specially commissioned by a Committee of the Corporation of Bury, a place where building leases are granted for terms of 999 years.

In the year 1887 a pamphlet prepared by Mr. Sidney Webb, and entitled "A Plea for the Taxation of Ground-rents," was issued by the "United Committee for Advocating the Taxation of Ground Rents and Values." The pamphlet is too slight and too violent in tone to be of material assistance in the investigation which is being undertaken in these pages. The main grievance alleged is that landowners have contrived to escape all direct taxation except income-tax*; and that while "the lease-" holder or intermediate landlord bears some share of " the rates—often, perhaps, the whole . . . the ground " landlord, who let the land at a fixed rent many years " ago, *bears no share whatever* of the unforeseen in- " crease of local taxation, even though his property

<small>Mr. Sidney Webb's pamphlet.</small>

---

* Mr. Webb is mistaken in stating that most occupiers have to pay the land-tax. In almost all cases land-tax is redeemed before building is commenced, because it is on annual value ; and in the remaining cases my experience has been that it is excepted from the rates and taxes to be borne by the lessee. Mr. Webb appears also to be in error in thinking that rates are divided between owner and occupier in the towns of Scotland and Ireland, if in the term "owner" he means to include receivers of feu-duties and ground-rents.

" be improved thereby." And the proposal made is (in addition to a proposal to tax vacant building land, which will be considered later on) that the occupier should be legally entitled to deduct from his rent one-half of the rates paid by him, and so that (apparently, as in the case of income-tax, by a series of deductions on the amounts of the rents successively paid) the owners of the "ground-values" should be reached. But no machinery is suggested by which ground-values are to be ascertained, or by which (if I have apprehended Mr. Webb rightly) the deductions would be prevented from falling on the owners of *building*-values, as well as of ground-values, in proportion to the rents they receive. I gather from a quotation from Burke at the beginning of the pamphlet that Mr. Webb considers it to be an additional argument in support of his proposals that owners as well as occupiers should be interested in the "maintenance of the community," in order that they may cease to be "in a sort separated from it."

An article in the "Westminster Review."

A much wider range of subjects, comprising indeed the whole general relative taxation of realty and personalty, is dealt with by an article in the *Westminster Review* for April 1888; but some attention is there given to the local taxation of ground-rents. It is alleged that surburban land is allowed to lie idle " solely with a view to the increase " in value which it will derive from the growth of " the towns;" that the landowner then lets the ground " at heavy ground-rents . . . free from assess- " ments, so far as he is concerned," and in respect of which " no charge whatever falls on the landowner;" and that the reasons for this state of things are, first, that " when the conditions of ownership of land in "this country were being determined" the nation did not understand the doctrine of "the unearned "increment of the land," in respect of which (until some scheme for its appropriation by the nation is devised) "the justice of demanding from the fortunate "owners substantial contributions to those rates "which are the life-blood of their growing fortunes "cannot be doubted," and, secondly, that "the "landowners, until recent years, usurped the entire "right to make laws, and constantly used this right "for their own advantage; in determining the method "of assessment of rates they departed from the "traditions of the country, which were to levy "charges on owners*; and, by causing the assess- "ments to be levied on occupiers, placed on their "tenants the burdens which they should have borne "themselves." And the remedy proposed by this writer is that, as in Cape Colony, rates should be assessed not on the rentals but on the values of all properties, and should be levied not on the occupiers but on the owners. But the proposal loses some practical value from the omission to state whether it is the whole ownership value of each house that is to be assessed or the values of the various interests in each house, and from the absence of any attempt in the latter case to indicate how the various interests are to be traced for purposes of valuation, and in the former case to define (a most important point) what the interest is which is to constitute a man the "owner."

* It seems, however, that from the first statutory imposition of the first rate—namely, the poor-rate, in the reign of Elizabeth—rates have always been levied on occupiers; and that this first statutory imposition followed existing practice as from the reign of Edward I. See Castle on Rating, chap. i.

Lord Hobhouse's proposals.

A very carefully written and moderately worded article is one contributed to the *Contemporary Review* for July 1888 by Lord Hobhouse, who was at that time the president of the "United Committee" before referred to. Lord Hobhouse's reason for advocating a change is clearly stated in the following passage:—

"Under the pressure of this actual large "increase of rates, and of the further increase "that is threatened, it is no wonder if Londoners "look about them to see what are the causes of "it, how the money is spent, and whether those "who benefit by it are made fairly to contribute "to it. They find that one potent cause of the "increase is the execution of works which effect "permanent improvements; some over a wider "and some over a narrower area. These works "increase the value of the owner's property. "But as such he pays nothing for them; the "whole charge falls on the occupier; and if by "chance the owner is himself the occupier, he "pays only as occupier and not as owner. Why "should we not bring in the owners to contribute "a fair share to the common expenses, in "consideration of the benefits they receive?"

Definition of term "owner."

Lord Hobhouse then goes on to carefully define the term "owner," since "many people imagine that "a proposal to throw a portion of the rates on "owners means that the portion is to be paid by "the ultimate reversioner or freeholder," a process that "would be very unjust, and probably very in-"efficacious too." When speaking of "owners" of

properties, Lord Hobhouse uses "a curt expression
" for all those persons who divide between them if
" more than one, or enjoy wholly if only one, the
" actual or estimated yield of such properties. Each
" of them should pay his quota towards that improve-
" ment or maintenance * of his property which is
" enforced by law." Lord Hobhouse then suggests
that " another point which requires elucidation is the
" amount of the expenditure which is applied to per-
" manent improvements," because this " makes the
" strongest part of the case for charging the owners,
" and . . . to this class of expenditure they should
" contribute a larger portion than to other classes."
But they ought also to contribute to other classes.
" If indeed all the rates were spent in the wants of
" the day, such as cleansing or lighting the streets, it
" might be just that the occupier, having enjoyed all,
" should pay for all." But in the case of such a rate
as the poor-rate, which is necessitated by the very
conditions which give value to the ground, owners
should, as deriving benefit, contribute. The principles
applicable to income-tax are applicable also to a poor-
rate and *a fortiori* to a rate for permanent improvements. An assessment of the capital value of every
separate interest in a house would both involve a
departure from present methods of taxation and be
unworkable in practice. The rates must in the first
instance, as at present, be paid by the occupiers, and
then they and every subsequent payer of rent must
deduct from that payment (as in the case of income-

* The word "maintenance" first slips in as coupled with
"improvement" in this passage, the argument so far having been
(as I understand it) only with regard to improvement. The great
importance of this addition will appear later.

E

tax) a proportion of the rates on that rent, which is fixed, " purely hypothetically," at one-fourth.

<small>Lord Hobhouse's views as to existing contracts.</small> Lord Hobhouse, however, here admits (what the previous writers have generally ignored) that a vast difference is made by contract, and states that up to this point he has been "treating the matter indepen-" dently of contract," and lays it down that as regards current contracts by the occupier to pay rates " this " bargain should not be disturbed without good and " clear cause being shown for it." But, on the whole, Lord Hobhouse considers that the recommendations of the Select Committee of 1870 are hardly adequate and would give " very little, if any, " relief to the occupier," * and proposes that in the case of contracts existing when the legislation he recommends is passed "the owner should be made " liable to bear his share of rates made for subsequent " permanent improvements," even apparently if those rates are not in excess of or are less than the rates for the same purpose when the contract was entered into.

<small>Mr. Moulton's pamphlet.</small> A rather different proposal has been made by Mr. J. Fletcher Moulton, Q.C., in a pamphlet entitled "The Local Taxation of Ground Values," which appears even more than Mr. Webb's pamphlet to be an authoritative exposition of the views of the " United Committee for Advocating the Taxation of " Ground Rents and Values." In Mr. Moulton's pamphlet the statement of the arguments for a change is not substantially different from the statements in the other writings which have been referred to, and

---

* In a discussion of this kind this argument seems wholly inadmissible. The object should not be " to give relief to the occupier," which may be conversely stated as " to cast a burden on the owner," but *to do justice between the parties.*

the novelty lies entirely in the suggested remedy. Mr. Moulton would in the case of the buildings in towns have separate and distinct valuations from time to time made (1) of the annual value of the sites on which the buildings stand and (2) of the annual value of the buildings themselves; and the occupiers should then be entitled to deduct the *whole* rates on so much of the annual value of their dwellings as represents the annual value of the ground, and these rates should by a series of deductions between the successive recipients of income from the buildings be thrown upon the recipients of all such rents as lie within the range of the ascertained annual value of the ground for the time being. And the reason of this rather complicated proposal is stated by Mr. Moulton in a subsequent defence of his plan to be that it is of no avail to attempt to throw rates on building rents directly on to the shoulders of builders, since, on the principles ordinarily applicable to the determination of the price of a manufactured commodity, they would throw the burden on to the shoulders of the consumers of the buildings—that is, the occupiers—and that therefore the annual value of the site is the only part of the rack-rent which it is of any purpose to rate directly.

As Mr. Moulton's proposal is of a peculiar character, needing a special and separate treatment which can hardly be given to it in the succeeding chapters, I may refer persons interested in this particular view to the number of the *Contemporary Review* for February 1890, which contains a criticism by me of Mr. Moulton's pamphlet, to a rather violent and personal reply by Mr. Moulton in the March number of the same periodical, and to a

This pamphlet treated elsewhere and in Appendix.

short rejoinder on my part which is contained in an
appendix to this essay. The main point which is in
my view established by this controversy is that Mr.
Moulton's proposal would not rate the *increase* of
ground-value, the whole of which does in fact go
into the pockets of the persons entitled either to the
possession or to the receipt of the *ultimate* values of
the house and site, but would instead rate the owners
of *fixed* rents, who do not benefit by the increase of
the ground-value (except so far as the capital value
of their rents is more or less increased) and whose
rents do in fact represent actual expenditure in
developing the land and building the houses—are in
fact the building rents, or in the nature of the building rents, which Mr Moulton declares it is of no
avail to rate.

Committee of London County Council.
In the month of June 1889 a Committee of the
London County Council, which had been appointed in
the preceding February "to consider the best method
" of ascertaining the value of land throughout the
" metropolitan area, irrespective of the value of
" buildings and of improvements made by the owners,"
issued a report together with minutes of the evidence
which had been taken before them. This report
relates rather to the question of taxing vacant building
land, which is not now under consideration, and even
so *assumes* the *principle* of rating vacant building
land on its capital value and deals only with the
feasibility of carrying out this principle. But some
of the evidence given before the Committee is of
considerable interest and importance on the question
of rating ground-rents; and there is annexed to the
evidence a very closely reasoned and in many respects
admirable report by the architect of the Council,

which will well repay attentive study. Reference may occasionally be made hereafter both to the evidence taken before this Committee and to the report of the architect.

Still more recently a Sub-Committee of the London County Council have been considering the incidence of local taxation in London with a view to the suggestion of some change. As Lord Hobhouse is the chairman of this Sub-Committee, it will probably be found that the views which he has promulgated in the *Contemporary Review* are largely adopted in their report. And it will be curious to notice whether the "purely hypothetical" one-fourth of the rates, which was in the article cast upon owners, has decreased to one-sixth or one-eighth, or has increased to one-third, one-half, or the whole, and whether the Sub-Committee have any more solid grounds than their chairman for suggesting the particular proportion that should be cast upon owners. It is much to be desired that if any definite proposal is made it will be justified by a process of as exact calculation as the nature of the case will allow, and that what is essentially a matter of business and finance will not be treated in a haphazard or happy-go-lucky spirit.

Sub-Committee of London County Council.

In concluding this chapter it may be pointed out that an idea which once prevailed has now been definitely exploded, namely, that the ground-rent of a house escapes rating at present, and would therefore form a fresh and hitherto " untapped " source of local taxation. The ground-rent of a leasehold house is included in and forms part of the annual value which is rated. And to rate such a ground-rent again would be to rate a part of the rent twice over,

All ground-rents are in fact rated already as part of the rack-rent.

and to impose to that extent a heavier rating on a leasehold house than on an adjoining freehold house. To rate ground-rents now means not to impose a rate on what was previously rated, but to force the owner of the ground-rent to pay the rate in spite of all future (and, under most proposals, of all past) contracts to the contrary.

CHAPTER V.

RATING AS BETWEEN BUILDING-OWNER AND OCCUPIER.

THE statement which has been made in the preceding chapter of the various proposals to cast the whole or a portion of the rates on owners in substitution for occupiers, or on one class of owners in lieu of another class, shows that by far the most important reason given for the proposed change is that the classes proposed to be rated do actually share with the classes now rated in the benefit of the expenditure of the rates, and that those who share the benefit ought also to share the burden. This reasoning of course implies that the classes proposed to be rated do not in fact already bear the burden which it is proposed to cast on them; but, subject to the proof of this assumption, there can be no doubt whatever of its cogency. An additional argument, though of far less weight, is that both the owner and the occupier *ought* as citizens to have a direct and immediate interest in the expenditure of the rates. And a third reason generally made use of is that local taxation has increased to a great and unexpected degree of late years. But this last argument seems valuable not so much directly as by way of rebutting any objection that may be taken on the ground of the inexpediency of interfering with existing contracts. When the subject is carefully examined it is by these

[margin: Summary of reasons for change.]

three main lines of argument that the proposals for change are justified, and of these by far the most important is the first, comprised as it is in the familiar legal axiom, "qui sentit commodum sentire " debet et onus."

Summary of practical proposal's for change.
In much the same way the practical proposals for change appear to narrow down upon examination. Attempts to value separately or to levy rates directly on the various interests of which the value of a house is composed are in general abandoned as impracticable; and the same remark seems to apply to any idea of ascertaining and rating the *capital* value of those interests. There appears, too, in all the proposals to be substantial accordance in this, that all rates are to be levied primarily on occupiers as at present, and are afterwards to be thrown either in whole or in part on the shoulders of those who are ultimately to bear them, by a series of deductions effected on the payment of rent similar to those with which everyone is familiar in the case of income-tax. Mr. Moulton's proposal is to relieve the occupier to the extent of the whole rates on so much of the rent as represents ground-value for the time being, and to throw the amount of which he is so relieved on the owners of the rents lying within that limit. But for the reasons I have mentioned I think that this proposal is quite mistaken and that it need not be separately further considered. The proposals of Mr. Webb and Lord Hobhouse, which are those to be practically considered, are that the occupier should be relieved from a larger or smaller proportion of the rates which he pays at present on the rack-rent, and that this amount should be rateably distributed over and deducted from every pound of annual income

received from house property. It is the object of the present and the succeeding chapters to examine how far these proposals are justified and how they would work in practice.

For this purpose it seems to be necessary in the first place to separate rather more distinctly than has been done hitherto the various interests which ordinarily exist in house property. The term "occupier" would appear not to be susceptible of any ambiguity, and yet it is often misleadingly applied to a person who is in fact an occupying owner—that is, who under the leasehold system is both in occupation and also the owner of the building-lease or building interest in the house. And, on the other hand, the word "owner" is sometimes used to denote the original freeholder of the property, who under the freehold rent-charge system would have become converted into a mere rent-charger, or under either of the leasehold systems would be the owner of the freehold ground-rent, including a more or less distant reversion; and is also often applied to the proprietor of the building interest who receives the rack-rent from the occupier, or to any other person who receives a share of the total annual rental which a house produces. Until these ambiguities have been cleared away it is almost hopeless to expect anything like a systematic investigation of the subject.

An analysis is necessary of the interests in houses.

In towns in England, at any rate, as the evidence before the Select Committee on Town Holdings has conclusively shown, it is quite the exception for the occupier to own the house he lives in or any large interest in it.* In towns developed on the freehold-

The occupier is seldom the owner.

---

* See the Report of the Select Committee, pp. 9 and 10. These parts of the Report appear to have been substantially adopted from Mr. Knowles' draft Report, paragraphs 51 to 56, but the Report strangely purchase system there are usually at least two interests in every house, namely, (1) the interest of the owning freeholder entitled to receive the rack-rent from the occupier, and (2) the interest of the occupier. And in towns built on the freehold rent-charge system or on either of the leasehold systems there are usually at least three interests in every house, namely, (1) the interest of the original landowner or of his successors in title, comprising either (*a*) a freehold rent-charge or (*b*) a freehold ground-rent, with the reversion at the end of 999 years or 99 years; (2) the interest of the builder or his successor in title, the " building-owner," comprising either (*a*) the freehold subject to a rent-charge or (*b*) a lease for 999 years or 99 years at a ground-rent, but in either case entitled to receive the rack-rent from the occupier; and (3) the interest of the occupier. Of course it very often happens that the interests in houses are even more numerous and complicated, inasmuch as (to take one instance) there is often, in addition to the first rent-charge or ground-rent representing the original value of the land, a second rent-charge (or " chief-rent ") or a second improved leasehold ground-rent, representing expenditure in the formation of streets and sewers and in general development. And in London, where values have a tendency to rise rapidly, there are often five or six interests in a house. But the intermediate interests may obviously for many purposes be regarded as subdivisions of the interest of the " building-owner," and the typical instance to be considered may be stated as one which in freehold-

omits to notice (as is done in Mr. Knowles' draft Report) what are the *terms* on which the actual occupiers hold from the owners of the buildings.

purchase towns results in two interests, and in towns under any of the other three systems results in three interests in every house.

In every town, therefore, the incidence of rates must be considered as between the owner of the rack-rent or "building-owner" and the occupier. And in every town not developed on the freehold-purchase system the incidence of rates must also be separately considered as between the "building-owner" and the owner of the annual payment representing the original value of the land, whom, for brevity, we will sometimes call the landowner. *Double aspect of the question of the incidence of rates.*

But the necessary subdivision does not even end here. We have seen that under the freehold rent-charge system and the Scotch feu system the interest of the landowner is absolutely limited for ever to the fixed annual payment which he has agreed to receive; and that under the 999 years system, although in theory the landowner has a reversion, in effect the reversion is so distant as to be of no value whatsoever, and his real interest consists, as under the two former systems, of nothing whatever beyond his present fixed annual rent. On the other hand, under the 99 years system, the landowner retains, in addition to his rent during the currency of the lease, a real reversion which begins to be felt within twenty or thirty years of the granting of the lease, and which, although of insignificant value for many years, gradually grows in importance until during the last years of the building-lease it becomes of much greater value than the present annual ground-rent; and when this reversion comes into possession it will clearly derive benefit from any improvements which may have been effected during the currency of the lease and which *A still further sub-division necessary.*

may still be of value. It will therefore be of great advantage if, when considering the incidence of rates as between "building-owner" and "landowner," a distinction is made between (*a*) landowners when and as they are the owners of fixed rents and (*b*) landowners when and as they are the owners of reversions, the interest of the landowner under the 99 years lease system being split up for purposes of calculation into its two component parts.

Three aspects of the question.

There are thus three aspects in which the incidence of rates will now be dealt with, namely: first, as between "building-owners" and occupiers; secondly, as between building-owners and the owners of fixed rents representing original land value; and thirdly, as between building-owners and the owners of reversions. The remainder of this chapter will be devoted to the first of these investigations.

The terms on which occupiers hold.

The terms on which occupiers hold from building-owners are not indicated in any part of the Report of the Select Committee on Town Holdings, but appear to be correctly stated in the following paragraphs of the draft Report proposed by Mr. Knowles:—

"57. . . . It would appear that in large
" towns the ordinary holding of labourers or
" artizans is a weekly tenancy, though they may
" occasionally hold on monthly, quarterly, or
" annual tenancies; and these long tenancies
" seem to be more common where there is a
" localised industry. Apparently the working
" classes are never known to hold on ordinary
" occupation leases, though an artizan may

" sometimes hold such a lease as a middleman
" for the purpose of sub-letting rooms.

" 58. With regard to shops, the smaller class
" seem often to be held on quarterly or even
" monthly tenancies, but the usual tenure for
" the ordinary class of shops seems to be an
" annual tenancy, and occupation leases for
" seven, fourteen, or twenty-one years are
" frequently taken, especially if values are rising.

" 59. With regard to dwelling-houses of the
" better class, tenancies are sometimes quarterly
" or half-yearly, but are more usually annual,
" and are very frequently, especially in the case
" of the larger houses, under occupation leases
" for seven, fourteen, or twenty-one years, but
" apparently hardly ever for a longer period,
" though Mr. Harrison thinks that occupation
" leases with over twenty years unexpired are
" common. The average length of the actual
" occupancy of these larger houses in London,
" as apart from the length of lease taken, has
" been estimated by Mr. Hunt, from his ex-
" perience of the Portman Estate, as not exceed-
" ing ten years."

The foregoing, then, being the general conditions on which occupiers hold from building-owners, it is next necessary to state precisely on whom the obligation to pay rates is primarily cast. From long before the 43 Eliz. c. 2 (which is " the basis but not " the origin" of the present system of parochial relief), and perhaps from as far back as the reign of Edward I., the obligation to relieve the poor, with which the other rates have from time to time been associated,

The persons directly responsible for rates by law.

has in general been cast upon the occupier and not upon the owner.* But particularly in modern times there have been established, partly by express enactment and partly by that custom which is the outcome of general convenience, many important exceptions to this rule.

<small>Owners of small houses, &c. made liable.</small>
By the 32 and 33 Vict. c. 41, following sec. 19 of the 59 Geo. III. c. 12, and the 13 and 14 Vict. c. 99, it is provided (section 1) that "the occupier "of *any* rateable hereditament let to him for a term "not exceeding three months shall be entitled to "deduct the amount paid by him in respect of any "poor-rate .... from the rent due or accruing due "to the owner;" (section 3) that "in case the rate- "able value of any hereditament does not exceed" £20 in the Metropolis, £13 in Liverpool, £10 in Manchester or Birmingham, or £8 elsewhere, the owner may compound for the payment of the poor-rate and be allowed a commission therefor; and (section 4) that in any case within the last section the vestry of any parish may order the owner to be rated to the poor-rate instead of the occupier, and shall in that case allow the owner certain alternative deductions.

<small>Owners more often liable than occupiers.</small>
I have no materials before me to show how far the provisions of this Act have been put in force, but it is common knowledge that this has been done to a very large extent †; and having regard to the facts already quoted as to the short tenancies on

---

* See the interesting historical account in the first chapter of Castle on Rating.

† Mr. Brevitt, in his evidence before the Select Committee on Town Holdings, said (1888—No. 1,869) that about two-thirds of the house property in Wolverhampton is compounded for.

which the working classes generally hold, and in view of the common practice amongst them of occupying rooms in tenement houses and industrial dwellings, where all rates are directly paid by the owner, there can be little doubt that it is the exception rather than the rule, especially in the central parts of large towns, for the working-class occupier to pay his rates directly. And even in the case of the wealthier classes the common practice of hiring furnished houses and the growing use which is made of flats and upper parts as residences, supply a large and increasing number of instances in which it is the owner and not the occupier who is rated. Add to all this the numberless cases in which persons live in furnished or unfurnished lodgings and pay a rent inclusive of rates to the occupier of the house, who is to them in the same position in which the building-owner is to the occupier, and I entertain little doubt that of the individuals and heads of families occupying separate holdings in London, and probably also in other large towns, only a small minority pay rates directly, and the great majority have their rates paid for them by their landlords.

The result is a startling one, and although it is fairly within ordinary experience it would be very desirable to have it tested by statistics which could probably be obtained from local authorities in various parts of the kingdom. But in the meantime, even without complete verification, the known facts are sufficiently important from at least three points of view. *Importance of this fact.*

In the first place it is quite clear that there is a very real and severe competition existing between tenements in which the occupier pays the rates and

Competition between tenements where owner pays rates and those where occupier pays.

those in which the owner pays the rates for him. And this fact, coupled with the ease and consequent frequency with which occupiers change their residences in town, must result in any increase of rates being quickly shifted on to the shoulders of the building-owner from those of the occupier.* Again,

Present practice based on general convenience.

it seems clear that the legislation and practice with regard to paying rates are alike based, not (as is alleged by Mr. Webb and other writers) on the principle of favouring the landlord class, but on that of general convenience to all persons alike. Where it is most convenient for the occupier to pay rates, he has to pay them; where it is most convenient for the landlord to pay, he pays them; but in no case are the trouble and worry of paying rates cast upon *both* the owner and the occupier as is now proposed.† And

Double-edged character of "citizenship" argument.

thirdly, the argument which is sometimes made use of, as in the resolutions of the Select Committee of 1870 and (impliedly) in Mr. Webb's pamphlet, that the owner as well as the occupier should, as a good citizen, be directly interested in the local taxation of the place in which his property is situate, seems to cut even more strongly the other way. An occupier seems to be even more directly interested than an owner in the local affairs of the district in which his house is situate. And the result of this process of reasoning would clearly be that in every single case

---

* In Mr. Goschen's draft Report presented to the Select Committee of 1870 it is pointed out that increases of local burdens are to some extent thrown on farmers, because (1) they hold at customary rents lower than rack-rents, and (2) it is difficult and unusual to apply for a reduction of rent, and inconvenient and expensive to remove. The first of these causes is non-existent in towns, and the second is reduced to a minimum.

† This point is further dealt with later on.

in which an occupier now has his rates paid for him by an owner, and in despite of every agreement to the contrary, the owner should be entitled to add to the rent and recover from the occupier an aliquot proportion of the rates which the owner has paid.

But now let us pass from the comparison of houses where the owner pays the rates with houses where the occupier is rated; and let us consider for the remainder of this chapter the latter class of houses only, with a view to discover if there is in fact any and what hardship in the occupier paying the whole of the rates. Consideration of the case where the occupier pays the rates.

Now here it is quite clear, in the first place, that the question is not in the least affected as regards the occupier by the building tenure on which the building-owner happens to hold. It is, indeed, often urged that in towns built, like London, on a comparatively short leasehold tenure there is a special grievance in the fact of the rates paid by the occupiers going to permanently enhance the value of the reversions of the freeholders. But this idea only arises from the common error (which has already been pointed out) of confusing the occupier with an occupying "building-owner." To the occupier pure and simple it can make no sort of difference in this respect whether the ownership of the house is in the hands of a single freeholder or whether it is split up into ten or twenty different interests. Indeed, it very often happens that the occupier is absolutely ignorant of the nature of the interest owned by the person to whom he pays rent. Any hardship on the score of tenure exists only as between the owners of the different interests in the house, and will be dealt with hereafter. The position of the occupier is precisely The tenure of the building-owner is immaterial.

F

the same in this respect in a freehold-purchase town like Wolverhampton, a freehold rent-charge town like Bristol, a 999 years leasehold town like Bury, or a 99 years leasehold town like Birmingham.

Any hardship is proportionate to the length of tenancies,

Again, the extent of any hardship must depend mainly on the length of the lease or tenancy under which the occupier holds. Any rates in force at the commencement of the tenancy are naturally taken into account when the terms of the tenancy are fixed, as has indeed been shown by some instances on previous pages of this work. And any increase in the rates paid by the occupier can only arise either from an increase in the poundage of the rates or from an increase in the rental value of the house he occupies. The latter alternative implies a gain to the occupier far exceeding the percentage of that very gain which he has to pay away in rates.* The former alternative does not practically take place to any great extent except over considerable periods of time. But the periods

which are usually short.

for which occupiers hold from building-owners are usually short, particularly in the case of the smaller classes of houses; and they hardly ever exceed, even in the case of the largest and most expensive houses, a period of twenty-one years, which is in most cases determinable by the occupier at the end of the first seven or fourteen years. And it follows, therefore, and indeed hardly seems to me to be in dispute, that as between the occupier properly so called and the building-owner of whom he holds there is not, in fact, any such increase during the period of the occupancy of the rates payable by the occupier as could on any

---

* Mr. Mathews pointed out in his evidence before the Select Committee on Town Holdings (1888 – No. 1,404) that in Birmingham "the "increment in ground-value has far outstripped the increment in rates."

hypothesis, and whether apart from contract or not, form any substantial grievance on the part of the occupier. And these considerations are, as will readily be perceived, entirely independent of the purposes to which the expenditure of the rates is devoted.

But when attention is directed to the manner in which the rates are in fact expended, the reason for levying the rates on occupiers is at once apparent. The vast bulk of the rates is expended in providing for the passing needs of the local community which the occupiers form. The lighting, cleansing, watering, and maintenance of the streets, the repair of the sewers, the provision of an adequate police, the maintenance of the aged and infirm poor, and the furnishing of education for the young—all these are modes of recurrent expenditure of which the benefit is reaped by the community for the time being, that is, by the occupiers. When to these are added, in towns where the gas-works and water-works have been acquired by the municipal authorities, the rates for the supply of gas and water, it becomes apparent that in many respects rates are merely payments made by the individuals composing the community for services, which it is more convenient that the community should supply to the individuals composing it than that these individuals should procure separately for themselves. And when it is remembered that the owner of a house may live in some completely different locality, in which he and the other members of the community there will have to provide the like advantages for themselves, it becomes manifestly inexpedient and unfair that he should be rated also in the locality in which his property happens to lie.

Rates mostly benefit the occupier;

and are in great part no burden at all.

Looked at indeed from this point of view, it is readily seen that a large proportion of the rates does not, in fact, form a *burden* at all, any more than the payment of a butcher's bill for meat supplied, or of a water company's rate for the provision of water, is a burden. The payment of such rates is in fact merely a payment for services rendered and to be rendered, and if the rates are properly expended a full equivalent is received by the ratepayers for their money. It is, of course, to the community of occupiers, not to the owners at all, that the services are rendered; and it is therefore obviously fair that the occupiers should pay in the first instance, however the payment may ultimately fall.

Any relief as to certain rates must be sought and is granted as between the nation and the locality.

It is, indeed, sometimes said that certain matters, such as the relief of the poor or the provision of elementary education, are not the concern merely of the occupiers in the locality in which the expenditure is incurred, but are of much more general importance, and should therefore be directly contributed to by owners. So far as these matters are of general importance it seems to me that the true solution is that they should be provided for, not by the owners of property in that locality, the result of which would be to impose a kind of local income-tax on one class of property only, but by the community at large. And this view has been sanctioned by the large and increasing contributions which are made out of imperial funds, not only to the general relief of local burdens, but in particular towards the expense caused by the provision of a system of national elementary education. The impracticability and unfairness of any attempt to levy a local income-tax which must almost necessarily be limited only to real estate have often been recognised, and nowhere more forcibly than in the following passage from a speech delivered by Mr. Goschen in the House of Commons on the 3rd April, 1871.*

"As regards the first method" (*i.e.*, of a local income-tax), "it appears to be impossible to devise an equitable local income-tax, for you cannot localise income. An attempt was made in Scotland, and it broke down when an English Lord Chancellor, who drew his £10,000 a year in London, but had a small place in Scotland, was made to pay income-tax on the whole of his income, in that country as well as in this. No country has been able to levy a local income-tax. In the United States there has not been a local income-tax, but a personal property-tax. What has been the result of that? A very able Report has just been published by Mr. Wells, who, with two other Commissioners, was appointed to inquire into its working. On the cover of that Report is this sentence:— [Local income-tax impracticable.] [American experience.]

'I insist that a people cannot prosper whose officers either work or tell lies. There is not an Assessment Roll now made out in this State which does not now tell and work lies.'

"In making the assessment to the personal property-tax, the oath of the person to be

* The passage is cited from Mr. Goschen's collected Reports and Speeches on Local Taxation, p. 204. Macmillan & Co., 1872.

"assessed is not questioned, and there is an
"instance adduced by Mr. Wells, on undoubted
"authority, in which a man assessed at $20,000
"swore he possessed only $15,000, and swore
"himself down $1,000 yearly, until in the year
"1869 he reached $1,000; in that year he died,
"and, as the Report expressed it, 'passed to
"'a tribunal where oaths could be inquired
"'into,' and his devised property was found to
"be worth $150,000. Mr. Wells concludes
"that the system is pregnant with fraud and
"perjury, and that the house a man lives in is
"the best test of what he can pay, pointing to
"England as offering a model system of local
"taxation, because it has adopted that test."

Present income-tax different.

The distinction between any such tax as this and the income-tax as we now experience it is obviously that the latter is levied upon all kinds of income alike, and by a central authority, the consequence being that it does not form a differential or preferential tax on one class of property, diminishing its value as compared with that of other classes.

Rates so far as falling on occupiers are a tax not on income but expenditure.

This last consideration leads naturally to some notice of the fact alluded to in the above quotation that, like almost all other taxes, rates are not, and are not regarded by political economists as, intended to tax income or property, but *expenditure*. Mill, who considers that a house-tax (which is his name for the rates and taxes on houses) falls ultimately on the occupier to "nearly all" its amount, also holds that it is one of the fairest of all taxes, inasmuch as there is on the whole no better test of a man's expenditure than the rent of the house he lives in.* This view has been attacked on the ground that the poorer a man is the greater is the proportion of his income which he spends in rent. But there are several considerations which weaken this last argument. For instance, in comparing the expenditure of the day labourer spending, say, 3s. 6d. a week in rent, with that of a professional man holding a house under a repairing lease at £150 per annum, it must always be remembered that the former rent is inclusive, not exclusive, of rates, and that after allowing for this and also for the allowances to a compounding landlord in respect both of his composition and of repairs (a very serious item), the net annual value on which rates would be levied would in the former case probably fall short of 2s. per week, while in the latter case it would very nearly amount to the full £150 per annum. Again, houses of less rental value than £20 per annum are relieved altogether from the payment of the important inhabited house duty of 9d. per £. Once more (altogether apart from the conclusion which has been arrived at in a previous chapter that a large proportion of rates on houses does in fact fall ultimately neither on the occupier nor the building-owner, but on the value of the site), in estimating the fairness or unfairness of the incidence of taxation as between different classes, it is the incidence of taxation as a *whole*, and not of one particular item, that has to be considered. And, finally, any adjustment that ought to be made on

* Mill's *Principles of Political Economy*, Book V. chapter iii. § 6 (p. 501. People's Edition, 1865). A house-tax is not nearly so oppressive a form of taxation to the poor as the *octroi* which forms so important a source of local revenue in many Continental countries

this score should be in the direction not of directly rating owners in lieu of occupiers, but in that of rating rather more lightly the smaller classes of houses.

Summary of conclusions of chapter. The argument in this chapter has ranged over so wide a field that it may possibly be useful to sum up in a few propositions the main conclusions that have been arrived at. Though all of them are claimed to be of some importance, the fact that many of them are merely replies to other arguments which have been urged in favour of a change prevents their presenting anything like a systematic exposition of the subject.

1. The incidence of rates between occupier and building-owner is in no way affected by the tenure of the house.

2. In the majority of cases rates *are* already paid directly by building-owners and not by occupiers, and this is particularly the case with the poorer occupiers.

3. This system of collecting from the owners in most cases is due to general convenience, which, and not the interest of any class, regulates the present system of rating.

4. General convenience prescribes that *either* the building-owner *or* the occupier should be troubled with rates, not both. If on grounds of citizenship the owner should be troubled where he is now free, the occupier should also on the like grounds be troubled where he is now free.

5. The short terms on which occupiers hold, the facilities for changing, and the competition with flats, &c., where the building-owners pay the rates, prevent increases in rates being thrown on occupiers in towns.

6. A large proportion of the rates is not strictly a *burden* at all, but merely a payment for services rendered to the occupiers.

7. Such rates as the poor-rate or the education-rate, which concern more than the local community, should be assisted, not by a local income-tax on certain kinds of property, but by contributions from national sources, as is now done.

8. Rates, like most other taxes, are, so far as they are paid by the occupier, a tax, not on income, but on expenditure measured by style of living, and are in this respect a fair tax.

CHAPTER VI.

RATING BETWEEN BUILDING-OWNERS AND THE OWNERS OF FIXED RENTS.

The result of the last chapter does not conclude this question.

THE question having been discussed in the last chapter whether any change in the present system of rating is desirable as between the occupier and the building-owner, it now becomes necessary to consider whether any such change can be properly demanded as between building-owner and landowner. For it by no means follows either that the grant of any relief to the occupier against the building-owner need involve a corresponding relief of the latter as towards the landowner, or that the negative conclusion which has been arrived at with regard to the first question need involve a negative answer to the second. There may be no reason for expressly throwing the rates, or any part of them, on the building-owner instead of the occupier, because any increase in rates can under existing circumstances be promptly shifted by the occupier on to the building-owner. But this very fact may give the building-owner the right to claim contribution against the landowner to the extent to which the latter may share in the benefit accruing from the expenditure of the rates without at present defraying his just share of them. And although the current proposals on the subject embrace the deduction of the whole or a part of the rates from *every* payment of rent, so as to give relief between the occupier and the building-owner as well as between the building-owner and the landowner, the reasoning by which these proposals are supported seems to point mainly to relief between the building-owner and the landowner. Indeed, in the case of current contracts, with regard to which the main stress of the conflict seems to lie, it is only between building-owner and landowner that any substantial relief seems capable of being granted, since as between building-owner and occupier the shortness of existing contracts and the frequency and ease of change of residence would quickly bring matters back to their former condition.

In investigating this subject, however, it is necessary for complete clearness, as was stated in the last chapter, to eliminate the disturbing influence of any substantial reversion. And accordingly the case primarily considered will be one under the freehold rent-charge system, the Scotch feu system, or the 999 years system, under the first two of which there is no reversion at all, and under the last of which there is no tangible or measurable reversion, left in the landowner. If and so far as a case under the 99 years system is examined, it will be only in respect of that part of the interest of the landowner which consists in a ground-rent during the currency of the building-lease, not in respect of that part of his interest which comprises the reversion on the expiration of the lease. The question of a reversion will be dealt with in the next chapter.

Exclusion of reversion.

The problem may, then, be shortly stated thus: When a landowner has parted with his land for building purposes, not for a lump sum but for a fixed

Problem stated.

rent-charge or ground-rent, should that rent-charge or ground-rent contribute according to its amount to the whole or a part of the rates levied on the buildings? It seems to me that justice and expediency alike demand that a decided negative should be given to this question for the reasons I am about to state.

The ground-rent has already paid rates.

In the first place the rent-charge or ground-rent in question has been shown in a previous chapter to have *already* suffered a deduction in respect of, and borne by anticipation very much more than, the full rates on its own amount, so far as such rates could be reasonably anticipated. The rates so borne by the rent-charge or ground-rent have, after an elaborate inquiry and in accordance with the views of leading political economists, been ascertained to be (1) the whole rates on the ground-rent itself, (2) the "differential" rates on the building-rent, and (3) some small proportion of the "constant" rates on the building-rent. And to proceed to impose *de novo* on the rent-charges or ground-rents in question the whole or any part of the rates on their annual amount would be merely to repeat in part without any justification a process which has been already gone through, at any rate so far as regards rates existing at the date of the creation of these rent-charges or ground-rents or capable of being reasonably anticipated at that time.

Express covenant by lessee to pay is universal.

Again, the universal practice in all these cases is for the grantee or lessee to expressly covenant in the widest terms to pay and discharge all rates and taxes whatsoever, and to indemnify the landowner therefrom. This is an essential part of the bargain between them given for good consideration and, according to the evidence of experts, expressly taken into account when the other terms of the bargain are fixed. The building-owner is to obtain all future increment in the value of the property and to run all risks with regard to it; the landowner is never to share in this increment, but is, on the other hand, always to receive his annual payment undiminished. And this being so, it seems to me that the contract is one which, on every principle of justice and finality in these matters, ought to be supported; and that at any rate, if it is reopened at all, it must be reopened generally,* and not merely in one of its terms for the express purpose of benefiting the building-owner at the expense of the landowner.

But it is said that building-owners are not free agents in their contracts with landowners and have this covenant to pay all rates and taxes forced on them; and also that there have of late years been unexpected increases of rates, such as could never have been foreseen by building-owners when they entered into their contracts. Now, such is the competition between different towns in the kingdom that I very much doubt whether there is in fact any place where landowners are enabled to impose any terms they please on builders or building-owners without giving them a full equivalent. But at any rate it is undoubted fact that in the great majority of places there is no such monopoly at all, and that in a large number of places there is the very keenest competition between landowners to attract building to their estates. And therefore it seems quite clear that the *universality* of the practice for building-

This is not the effect of monopoly.

* See the very clear and definite evidence to this effect given by Mr. Eccleston Gibb before the Land Valuation Committee of the London County Council.

owners to covenant to pay rates and taxes cannot be the effect of monopoly but must depend upon some general perception of the fact that such a covenant is a fair and equitable one.

Impossible to guess how far increase in rates has been foreseen.

With regard to the question whether building-owners have or have not foreseen increases of rates, it seems to me impossible to enter into a speculative inquiry of this kind. They expressly took all the risk, and it is quite as likely that the amounts of future rates may have been over-estimated in some cases as underestimated in others. It is not as if such covenants were entered into only in past times, when rates are stated to have been low (though, taking into account the amount of services rendered in return for them, this may well be doubted), and have been abandoned now that rates have shown a distinct tendency to increase. Such covenants are as freely and invariably entered into to-day as ever they were. Can it be said that builders and building-owners making bargains to-day have no notice that rates are likely to increase? And what increase is to be laid down as that which they may reasonably be expected to anticipate? Or is it to be laid down as an axiom that no bargain ought ever to be made that the owner of one interest in land shall receive all the increase, and in return covenant to provide the owner of another interest with a fixed payment participating neither in any increase nor in any decrease? It would be as reasonable to enact that the holders of debenture stock in a railway must not receive a fixed or invariable income, but must from time to time pay some proportion of the varying working expenses of the railway, or at any rate a proportion of the varying rates which are from time to time imposed on the real estate of the railway and which now fall exclusively on the ordinary shareholders.

The nature of the hardship that would be inflicted by any legislation that should rate existing rent-charges or ground-rents would also be much aggravated through the class of persons who have purchased and hold them. With regard to this a quotation may be made from my former book, which has been amply borne out by the evidence before the Select Committee on Town Holdings:—* Great hardship would result from a change in the law,

" Although on many of the large residential
" estates in and about London the ground-rents
" are still held in one hand, in many other dis-
" tricts ground-rents are almost infinitely
" subdivided amongst purchasers and sub-
" purchasers from the original owners. These
" purchases have, in a very large number of
" cases, been made at public auctions, where the
" holders of the ground-leases subject to the
" ground-rents have had an opportunity (which
" they have not taken) of purchasing these ground-
" rents and thus acquiring the fee-simple of
" their houses. The purchasers, again, are of
" every grade of society, and do not in any
" marked degree consist of those who are some-
" times styled the 'landowning classes.' They
" are often not landowners at all, except in
" respect of the particular ground-rents they
" have purchased. not to "landowners" only, in the ordinary sense,

* See the Report of the Committee, pp. 31 and 32. The Birkbeck Building Society was stated by Mr. Martin (1887, No. 1,958) to have £200,000, and the Prudential Insurance Company by Mr. Gregory (1887, No. 3,491) to have £1,300,000, invested in these securities.

but to small and prudent investors.

"But, further, these investors are of a class
"who are content with a small return on their
"capital, so long as they can obtain a fixed
"income and perfect security. They are the
"same class who invest in Consols, in corpora-
"tion stocks, in the debenture and preference
"stock of first-class railways, and in other high-
"class securities of the same description. Trus-
"tees, retired professional men, spinsters, fire
"and life assurance companies of all kinds,
"and, in fact, all persons and corporations who
"require an income well secured, fixed, and
"free from trouble and anxiety, form the bulk
"of the investors in ground-rents.

Enormous loss that would ensue.

". . . . . .
"Now, taking rates at an average of 4s. or
"5s. in the £, the effect of rating ground-rents
"would be to take from this class of investors
"from 20 to 25 per cent. of their incomes, while
"the capital value of their property would pro-
"bably be yet more seriously injured. A more
"cruel and wanton interference with a most
"deserving class of persons it would be difficult
"to imagine. An instance may be mentioned
"which has recently come to my knowledge,
"and which is only typical of thousands of
"others. A professional man, with several
"unmarried daughters, has provided for them
"by investing the whole of the savings of a life's
"hard work in the purchase of ground-rents.
"The passing of a measure for the rating of
"ground-rents will deprive these ladies of a
"fifth, a quarter, or an even more considerable
"proportion of their incomes.

"The wrong done will, in fact, be the more cruel the smaller the investor. The wealthy nobleman, with £50,000 a year from ground-rents, can be mulcted of £12,500 a year, and yet be reasonably well off, though this would not, of course, justify the robbery. But the spinster or widow with an income of £100 a year from ground-rents cannot submit to a deprivation of one-fourth of her income without the extremest hardship." (pp. 146 to 150.)

Having seen who would suffer by the proposed change, it may be well also to note who would be the chief gainers. It will be in the memory of all who were interested in the cognate subject of leasehold enfranchisement that it was at length appreciated how entirely the result would be to enfranchise not the occupier but the middleman, especially in the case of the poorer occupiers, and that immediately this conviction took root all popular enthusiasm for a measure which never rested on any solid foundation of reasoning began to disappear. Curiously enough, the analogous scheme for the taxation of ground-rents, which also at first sight appears to be an occupiers' measure, and has gained a large share of public favour on this ground, also proves on further examination to be calculated to benefit not occupiers but building-owners—particularly in the case of buildings occupied by the poorest classes. Even in well-to-do neighbourhoods, where rates are paid in the first instance by the occupiers, it has been seen that building-owners will probably soon get the benefit of any remissions of rates on the readjustment of terms that is perpetually taking place. But a much more direct and

The chief gainer would be the middleman.

obvious advantage will be reaped by the middleman who compounds for his rates and farms out single rooms to the very poor at weekly rents, inclusive of all rates. For while he will be relieved at the expense of his landlord of the payment of a portion of the rates, there will be no reason whatever for his charging his tenants one penny less than he has hitherto done. It is probable that when this aspect of the case has once impressed itself (as it cannot fail to do) on the popular mind, the unreasoning enthusiasm for some change which at present prevails amongst persons quite unfitted to understand the economical bearings of the question will immediately subside, and that the matter will be left to be determined on the dry economical foundation on which I am at present endeavouring to build. Towards a consummation so devoutly to be wished nothing can assist better than the enforcement of the axiom that *the rating of ground-rents means the relief not of the occupier but of the middleman.*

Who *ought* to bear the rates?

So far in this chapter the case primarily urged has been that of the owners of existing rent-charges and ground-rents who have made their bargains in the past, and may reasonably complain of these bargains being revised in the future, especially in one item only, and exclusively to their disadvantage. But the last sentence of the last paragraph leads naturally to the consideration of the general relations of the building-owner to the landowner whose interest has been commuted into a fixed rent-charge or ground-rent. Altogether apart from the grave injustice and inexpediency of upsetting existing contracts, who *ought* to bear existing and future rates? Should they be borne exclusively by the building-owner, or should the landowner contribute to them in proportion to the amount of the fixed annual payment which he receives?

I cannot entertain a doubt that in this respect universal custom is in accordance with justice and expediency, and that the *whole* of these rates ought to be borne by the building-owner. He and he alone is entitled to the whole of the benefit of the expenditure of the rates, and to the whole of any value which may hereafter accrue to the land. The landowner does not receive a *fixed proportion* of the profits of the building and land whatever they may be (in which case it would be quite right, apart from contract to the contrary, that, as sharing any benefit, he should also share any burden), but a fixed annual sum insusceptible of any fluctuation in the direction of increase, and therefore properly saved from any fluctuation by way of decrease. He is a mere chargee or incumbrancer on the land and building, and not in any true sense the *owner* of any part of the property any more than a mere annuitant or mortgagee. {The building-owner ought to bear the whole.}

Let us pursue this last analogy a little more closely, and consider what *real* difference there is between a landowner who has sold a plot of land for building purposes for £250 and has allowed the price to remain on mortgage of the land and building at 4 per cent., and the landowner who has sold an equivalent plot for an annual rent-charge of £10, calculated as being at the rate of 4 per cent. on the capital value. It is conceded on all hands that in the first case the landowner should not be rated on the interest of his £250 mortgage debt; and this, as I understand it, not merely because his mortgage {Analogy with the case of a sale and mortgage.}

might be called in (many mortgages cannot in fact be called in till the expiration of fixed periods), or because the result would be to at once raise the interest on such mortgages to the extent of the rates levied, but because the mortgagor and not the mortgagee is the true owner of the land, and is entitled to all the benefit to be derived from expenditure on it. For instance, a report in the *Oracle* of the 7th December 1889 of an interview with Mr. Moulton on the taxation of ground-values contains the following passage on the subject :—

"With regard to allowing for mortgages, in
"considering the taxation that ought to be paid
"by town lands, Lord Salisbury seems to have
"forgotten that mortgages are only the securities
"for debt, and one cannot see why a man should
"pay less for property, *the whole improvement of*
"*which by the community he enjoys*, merely
"because he has debts against which that
"property stands as security. The principle of
"my proposition is, that we should follow the
"annual land value into whatever hands it
"comes, and tax it there, for it is a product, to
"a large extent, of that very expenditure to
"which this taxation ministers."

<small>Mortgages are exactly analogous in this respect to fixed rents.</small>

With the reasoning in this passage, so far as regards mortgages, it is impossible not to agree. The whole benefit of any increase in the mortgaged property goes to the mortgagor, not to the mortgagee, and therefore it would be unjust (as well as inexpedient and in a short time futile) to attempt to levy rates on the interest of a mortgagee in house property. But where is the difference in this respect between mortgages and rent-charges or ground-rents, apart of course in the latter case from any reversionary value? Does not the reasoning in the one case apply with precisely equal force to the other? It is indeed said that rent-charges or ground-rents are *maintained* by the rates, if they are not *increased*. But the same is the case with a mortgage, since its security would be just as much affected by rates ceasing to be expended on the property. It is again said that the capital value of a rent-charge or ground-rent will be increased by an addition being made to the value of the house that it is charged on. But if it is already well secured the addition can be but trifling, and if it is ill secured the analogy to a mortgage again recurs, since the value of an ill-secured mortgage does not equal its nominal value, and increases with any increase of the security. And finally the personal covenant to pay which makes a mortgage a debt, though charged on land, is precisely paralleled by the personal covenant to pay a rent-charge or ground-rent which makes the recurrent payments in respect of it personal debts, though also charged on or issuing out of land. The analogy between mortgages on buildings and rent-charges or ground-rents issuing out of them is, to my mind, complete and satisfactory; and any reasoning which leads to the conclusion that mortgagees should be exempted from any payment of rates in respect of the property on which their mortgages are charged must, in my view, lead irresistibly to the analogous conclusion that the receivers of fixed rent-charges and ground-rents must, as such, be also exempted from any payment on the like account.

Indeed, when a close examination is made of the

Arguments from creation *and* maintenance *incompatible.*

argument that rents, or any part of them, should be rated because they are *created* and *maintained* by the rates, the incompatibility of the reasons implied in the two words which have been italicised becomes apparent. If the income derived from an investment is increased it may be reasonable to throw some burden, commensurate with that increase, on the man who receives the increase. But is the burden also to be thrown on every man who is already in receipt of a fixed income from that investment because his income is *maintained*? Such maintenance is necessarily implied in the increase of the ultimate income, and to rate for it as well as for the increase seems to be rating twice over in the course of the same process. And if the rating ought in some way to be divided between creation and maintenance, in what proportions ought this division to be made? In fact, this proposal to rate maintenance as well as creation of value, which is suggested by Lord Hobhouse and forms a prominent feature of Mr. Moulton's scheme, seems to originate in a confusion of ideas. If the expenditure of rates produces an equivalent increase, that increase should be *taken*, not *rated*, and should be taken, as is done at present, from the person who enjoys the increased value, not from the persons who receive a fixed value, ascertained before the increase took place. A good practical example of the kind is worked out in the Appendix.

A practical illustration.

The above chain of reasoning seems to me a complete answer to any proposal to charge any part of either present or future rates on any fixed rent-charge or ground-rent issuing out of a building; but the principle is so vital to the subject that it may be well to illustrate it by a definite example. Let us assume that A, a freeholder, has agreed to grant a considerable area of land to B for a rent-charge, which works out (when apportioned evenly) at a rent-charge of £5 for the site of each house; that B, having formed the roads and sewers and developed the land generally, agrees to grant off particular sites to builders, of whom C is one, at a rent-charge of £10 per site, thus becoming himself entitled to a second rent-charge or "chief-rent" of £5 net per annum; and that C has erected a house on his plot of the original net rental value, inclusive of the site, of £60. The position of the parties is then obviously the following:—A is entitled to a first rent-charge of the annual value of £5, B is entitled to a second rent-charge of the net annual value of £5, and C is entitled to the balance of the income which is obtained from the house. A and B are therefore each *at present* receiving one-twelfth of the income of the house; and if their interests were, in fact, defined as consisting of the right to receive one-twelfth of the income of the house for the time being, it might be proper that they should each pay one-twelfth of any expenditure that would increase that income. But the interests of A and B are not so defined, and do, in fact, consist of the right to receive *a fixed sum, not a fixed share*, out of the income of the house; and not five-sixths only but the *whole* of any addition to the income of the house will go into the pocket of C. If then large public improvements are suggested which will add 1s. in the £, or £3 in all, to the rating of the house in question, but which will also enhance the value of the house to the extent of £3

The rent-charger receives a fixed sum, not a fixed share.

or upwards, there seems no reason for charging any part of these rates upon A and B. For C will receive the *whole* of the extra rental value of £3 or upwards, and is therefore clearly the person on whose shoulders the whole of the £3 extra rate should fall. To charge, as is proposed, 1s. in the £ or 6d. in the £ on A and B would be to reduce the rates paid by C to £2. 10s. or £2. 15s. as the case may be, while allowing him still to take the benefit of the whole of the £3 or upwards forming the extra rental of the house and land.

Owners of fixed rents have no control over the expenditure of the rates.

Beside an obvious unfairness of this kind it is of comparatively slight importance to mention that A and B have at present no control whatever over the expenditure of the rates to which they would be called on to contribute. Taxation without representation, bad as it may be, does not strike one as quite so unjust as taxation for purposes in the benefit of which the person taxed does not share. But it should nevertheless be observed that any such change in the incidence of taxation must be accompanied or preceded by a change in local representation, which would give the owners of fixed rent-charges and ground-rents an opportunity of voting on questions connected with the imposition and expenditure of local taxation ; and it is quite obvious what an obstacle would be presented to local improvement and local progress by the introduction of a large class of voters, who would naturally object to any increase of expenditure to which they would have to contribute but in the benefit of which they would not be allowed to share.

Future transactions.

Once more, the effect must be considered which legislation of this kind will have on future transactions. No doubt in future the tendency will be for rent-charges and ground-rents to rise to the extent to which rates are cast upon them, both because the occupier will to that extent offer a higher rack-rent, on which, as we have seen, the ground-rent depends, and also because ground-rents on the building limit, which only just tempt the landowner at present to divert his land from agricultural or accommodation purposes, will have, after the change, to rise to at least the extent of the rates imposed on them before they will so tempt him in the future. And so far the effect will be to just counterbalance any tax imposed on the landowner. But beyond this there can be little doubt that a change which will in effect declare that no income whatever, when derived from buildings, shall be free from the trouble and variability caused by deductions in respect of fluctuating rates, will drive out all cheap or trust capital from this method of investment into the debenture and preference stocks of railway companies and other like securities, which return an income small indeed, but free from fluctuation or trouble. The point is well stated by Mr. Beken, a well-known dealer in ground-rents, in the following passage, at page 31 of a little pamphlet which he has styled " Freehold " Disfranchisement":— *[margin: Cheap capital will be driven out of house property,]*

" I consider that such a system would, by
" increasing the trouble or cost of management,
" diminish the value of the property as a whole,
" from which some, if not all—and I think all—
" the parties would suffer.
" The income-tax on ground-rent increases.
" probably sometimes doubles, the trouble of

"collection; but this trouble is trifling com-
"pared with what would be caused by a similar
"system for local rates. The rate of income-
"tax in the £ is the same for the whole year;
"it is also the same for every parish; and it
"seldom consists of a mixed number (*i.e.*, a
"whole number and a fraction). The rate per
"£ is, therefore, known to all parties without
"the production of receipts or other evidence,
"and it is quickly calculated. The local rates,
"however, vary not only within the year—as
"an example, 1s. 2¾d., 1s. 2¾d., 1s. 3½d., 1s. 3½d.,
"for the four quarters respectively—but they
"vary with each parish, and they are often
"represented by mixed numbers. Evidence of
"the rates per £ must therefore be produced
"for each deduction on rent paid between the
"parties (say, between the tenant, perhaps one
"or more under-lessees, the lessee, and the
"freeholder). In addition, most payments
"would necessitate a fractional calculation—for
"example, £2. 10s., £3 15s., £5, and the like,
"at 1s. 2¾d. in the £—simple enough no doubt
"for every one, but all taking time. Parties
"would be deterred by an objection to niggling
"details from making arrangements for sub-
"dividing their interests which would other-
"wise be mutually advantageous, capital would
"be diverted from the creation of property, and
"the employment of labour thereby checked,
"and all for what?"

and rents will be raised.

An example will show how, if ground-rents are lowered in capital value through increased trouble and cost in collection and variability in income, rack-rents must necessarily rise. Let us assume the case of a landowner on the building limit, who is just prepared to part with his land for a capital sum of £200 per acre, or £50 for the site (which we will estimate at one rood, less roads) of each villa to be built; and let us further assume that the cost of formation of roads and sewers, and development of the land generally, will also be at the rate of £200 per acre. If then first ground-rents will at present sell at 25 years' purchase, and second or leasehold ground-rents at 20 years' purchase, the landowner will be content with a ground-rent for himself of £2 per site, and the intermediary who develops the land will be content with a further rent of £2 10s. per site, the capital value of each of these rents being £50. But if, through the causes above mentioned, the price of a freehold ground-rent sinks to 20 years' purchase, and that of a leasehold ground-rent to 16 years' purchase, the landowner must get a ground-rent of £2 10s., and the intermediary a second or leasehold ground-rent of £3 2s. 6d., before it will be worth the while of the one to let or of the other to develop; and thus no less than £1 2s. 6d. per annum is at once added to the ground-rents payable on the house. It will be observed that in this example no addition has been supposed to be made to the two ground-rents (as would no doubt be the case) to cover the rates they will have to bear, because, as the occupier will be relieved to this extent, this amount will not be a real addition to the rack-rent of the house. But the extra ground-rent which will have to be provided to compensate for the diminished value of these securities as an investment, owing to the increased trouble of collection and the variability of the income derived from them, will form a real addition to the rack-rent of the house for which there will be no compensation.

Summary of contents of chapter. It may now be well at the close of this, as of the previous, chapter to sum up concisely the reasons which render unjust and inexpedient the proposals to shift rates, or any part of them, from the building-owner to the owner of a fixed charge or ground-rent, either in the case of present or in that of future contracts. They are as follows:—

As regards existing contracts:

1. Upon the ascertainment of existing rent-charges and ground-rents rates have already been deducted from them to an extent far exceeding the rates on these rent-charges or ground-rents themselves.

2. The building-owners have for good consideration entered into an express contract with the owners of these fixed rent-charges or ground-rents to defray *all* the rates.

3. This contract is a reasonable and proper one, not forced on the building-owners, and it is impossible to say whether the rates actually existing are greater or less than those estimated.

4. The most prudent and deserving classes of investors would be mulcted of a considerable part both of the income and of the capital of their investments by the proposed change.

5. The result of the change would be, especially in the poorest quarters, to benefit not the occupier but the middleman.

As regards future contracts:

6. The proposed change would not produce any relief, since it would result in a rise of rent-charges and ground-rents for building land at least equal to the amount of rates they would have to pay.

7. The utmost difficulty and trouble would be caused by the various deductions and allowances that would have to be made as between every payer and receiver of rent.

8. In consequence of this difficulty and of the necessary variability of every income derived from town holdings, all cheap and trust capital would be driven from investment in buildings, and rents would rise.

And as regards both existing and future contracts:

8. The owner of a building subject only to a fixed rent-charge or ground-rent is the owner of the whole interest, and not only of a part, just as if he held subject only to a mortgage. He will take the whole and not merely a proportion of every benefit to the building, and he should therefore discharge the whole and not merely a porportion of every burden on the building.

CHAPTER VII.

RATING BETWEEN BUILDING-OWNERS AND THE OWNERS OF REVERSIONS.

<small>What difference is caused by a reversion?</small>
A VERY definite conclusion has so far been arrived at that, as between building-owners and the owners of fixed rent-charges and ground-rents, it would be unjust in the case of existing contracts, and inexpedient in the case of future contracts, to relieve the former class of any portion of the rates at the expense of the latter class. It is still necessary to inquire whether any difference in this respect is caused when the owner of the ground-rent is also the owner of a tangible reversion—that is, when the term of years for which his ground-lessee or building-owner holds is so comparatively short that there is some real measurable prospect of the landowner resuming possession of his land, with the building on it. For in this case the interest of the landowner is obviously not limited to a fixed payment wholly irrespective of any subsequent value that may be added to the site and building. He will be entitled at the expiration of the building-lease to the site itself with the building on it, and therefore to any improvement or added value that may have accrued to it through (amongst other things) the expediture of the rates.

<small>Some rates are spent on permanent improvements.</small>
Now, it is unquestionable that a certain proportion of the rates is expended upon objects of a more or less permanent character. The open spaces that

are from time to time provided, the new arterial streets
that are constructed, and such great works as those of
which the Thames Embankment is the most striking
instance, may all be fairly regarded as adding an
entirely permanent value to the land of the Metropolis. Even such less permanent improvements as
the main drainage system, the freeing of the bridges
over the Thames, the provision of great prisons and
lunatic asylums and of the legion of elementary
Board schools which have sprung up of late years,
will, however much reconstruction and modification
may from time to time be required, outlast to a large
extent the currency of the leases during which they
have been constructed and paid for. And the consciousness that to this extent the London landowner
will, on the expiration of his building-lease, step into
the enjoyment of an enhanced value, to the creation of
which he has not directly contributed, lends added
force to the proposals to rate that present ground-rent which is incident to, and will at last disappear
into, his reversion.

Unhappily, from the point of view of rating that
which is really benefited, namely, the reversion, these
proposals are both illogical and unsatisfactory. Not
only would they involve rating improved leasehold
ground-rents which are terminable, involve no real
reversion as a rule, and mostly represent actual
expenditure on the development of land and on
building,* but they would also rate reversions on

<small>Current proposals fail to deal with this.</small>

<small>* Mr. Moulton's plan is particularly unsatisfactory in this respect. On an increase in ground-value he would rate, not the rack-rent which receives the whole increase, but the initial or bottom rents which (1) remain fixed and (2) represent former outlay in development and building. And yet, strangely enough, he lays great stress on the practical futility of attempting to rate building-rents.</small>

the basis of the arbitrary ground-rents paid to the landowner, and without regard either to the proximity of the reversion or the proportion of the rates spent in permanent improvements. Under the operation of these proposals a freehold ground-rent of £10 per annum, with a reversion to occur in ninety years, would incur rates to ten times the extent of a freehold ground-rent of £1 per annum on a precisely similar house, with a reversion to occur in one year; though it is obvious that any expenditure of the rates on improvements must benefit the interest of the landowner in the latter house much more directly and substantially than the owner of the reversion of the other house. Again, a leasehold ground-rent on either house of £20 per annum would pay rates to a greater extent than either of the freehold ground-rents, though it would never receive any reversionary benefit at all from any of this expenditure. And the same proportion of the rates would be levied on all these ground-rents, whether one-hundredth or one-half of the expenditure of these rates was devoted to purposes calculated to increase reversionary value. In fact, no definite proposal of any practical value has yet been put forward for the rating of reversions.

There is a small but inevitable hardship apart from contract.

This last fact, however, seems rather to indicate that there are practical difficulties in the way than that there is, in fact, no anomaly to be investigated. And while I hold strongly that from every point of view the rating of *present* ground-rents and rent-charges would be as indefensible as the rating of mortgages, I think, on the other hand, that there is, apart from contract, a distinct hardship in the landowner receiving, on the occurrence of his reversion, a benefit arising from expenditure to which he has not contributed. But I also think that the grievance is far less in extent than is generally considered; that there would be insuperable practical objections to any plan for taxing these reversions; and accordingly that as well general convenience as the ordinary form of contract, which is in almost all cases the outcome of general convenience, prescribes that the whole of the rates should fall on the present rack-rentals of house property and that no part of the rates should be charged against reversionary value. But inasmuch as this result depends not on an ascertainable and definite principle, but on considerations of the balance of convenience, it is essential to estimate as accurately as possible both the extent of the hardship in question and the difficulties that surround any attempt to remedy it.

In the first place, the grievance in question does not appear to be an occupier's grievance. Occupiers hold under the same conditions in leasehold as in freehold towns; they are not affected by, and are often ignorant of, the fact whether the houses they occupy belong entirely to one person or are subdivided into a number of different interests; and besides, they have frequent opportunities of adjusting with their immediate landlords the conditions of their tenancies. It is rather the building-owners who are prejudiced by suffering a diminution, or failing to obtain an increase, of rent to the extent of the rates which go to benefit the reversion. The question, therefore, is one between two sets of capitalists—not between a set of capitalists and the public. This fact does not of course obviate or diminish any hardship that exists. But it is well to clear the ground before

The hardship has nothing to do with the occupier.

H

starting of any false impression of the kind which might otherwise perhaps tend to exaggeration or prejudice.

<small>Special areas must not be considered alone.</small> Again, it is unfair for the present purpose to direct attention exclusively to certain special areas which have been extraordinarily improved by the expenditure in their vicinity of the concentrated rates of the whole Metropolis, without also considering the far larger areas which either derive no substantial benefit whatever from the expenditure or may even be deteriorated by it through the diversion of traffic * and other like causes. It is improper to use the manifest improvement which has accrued to land south of the Strand through the construction of the Thames Embankment to justify a proposal to rate reversions throughout the Metropolis, including reversions to property at Kilburn or Holloway which has probably been entirely unaffected by the work. Such instances rather raise the question of the special taxation of specially benefited areas or " betterment," a subject outside the scope of the present treatise, but which seems to bristle with practical difficulties and to be likely, if treated with anything like logical accuracy, to lead to the decentralisation and disintegration of the various Metropolitan districts which have so lately been welded together under a centralised authority. No proportion of the rates can be levied on reversions throughout the Metropolis generally except to the extent to which there has been a general average improvement in reversions due to the expenditure of the rates.

* Complaint has for instance been made of the damage that has thus been done to shops in St. Martin's Lane by the construction of Charing Cross Road.

Once more, the grievance in question does not extend to the whole rates levied on houses, but only to such part of them as is expended in such a manner as to benefit the reversion; and it therefore becomes necessary to estimate as between the building-owner and the reversioner what proportion of the rates is, in fact, so expended. Now, it is within the knowledge of every ratepayer that by far the larger part of the rates is devoted to current annual expenditure, which is exhausted within the year and confers no benefit upon the owners of reversions. The money spent in the lighting and repair of the streets, the maintenance of sewers, the preservation and regulation of parks and open spaces, the provision of an efficient police force, and many other items of this character, is spent as strictly in satisfying the recurrent needs of the community, and leaves as little permanent benefit behind to property, as the sums spent by individuals in food and drink. And the same appears also to be the case with the ordinary annual expenditure of the poor-rate or the education-rate, the provision of which in any year is for the purposes of that year only and does not obviate or diminish the necessity of making a similar provision in succeeding years. It is obvious, therefore, that for this part of the rates building-owners or occupiers can have no claim whatever against the owners of reversions. Indeed, an excellent *reductio ad absurdum* of the opposite view was afforded by the evidence before the Select Committee on Town Holdings of an Irish witness who estimated at £2,000,000 or upwards the whole amount of the rates and taxes that would be paid by the tenants on the De Vesci estate during 99 years, and inferred that the ground land-

The hardship only extends to a small part of the rates.

Robinson (1886), 974-984.

lord would be ultimately benefited by the expenditure of the whole of this enormous sum, probably many times exceeding the whole value of the estate when it should fall into possession.

Example. It is then only so far as rates are levied to defray expenditure upon objects of permanent value and utility that reversioners are benefited by their expenditure. Such objects are usually provided for by borrowing, on the security of the rates, the requisite capital sums; and there is then provided out of the rates an annual sum sufficient to pay off these sums, together with interest on the parts for the time being unpaid, in a period of about fifty years. Let us assume that in this present year, 1890, some very important object of this kind is provided for at an annual charge on the rates of 4*d*. in the £ (of which 3*d*. represents interest and 1*d*. sinking-fund) spread over the next fifty years, and let us consider to what exact extent reversioners will be benefited at the expense of building-owners.

The interest on loans for improvements does not benefit the reversioner; To the extent of the 3*d*., which represents interest on the loan in question, it seems clear that the reversioner derives no benefit, and ought not to contribute anything. It is the persons having immediate interests in the building who enjoy for the time being the advantage of the improvement, and they should therefore provide the interest on the capital outlay necessary to furnish the improvement as much as the annual expense of maintaining it in order. Or, to look at it from another point of view, if there were no sinking-fund at all, but only the 3*d*. annual charge necessary to keep down the interest of the loan, and even assuming the effects of the improvement to be absolutely permanent, the reversioner would obtain

no benefit from the expenditure on the occurrence of
the reversion; since, although on the credit side of
the account he would have the improvement, on the
debit side he would have outstanding the capital
debt which had been incurred for the purpose of
providing the improvement.

As to the 1*d*. which represents the sinking-fund *and only a part of the sinking-fund.*
in respect of the improvement in question, the case
is different. Assuming indeed that the duration of
the improvement were exactly co-extensive with the
period of operation of the sinking-fund, it seems that
the whole of the sinking-fund as well as the interest
would be properly chargeable against the building-
owner. And assuming that the period of operation
of the sinking-fund were so spread out as to outlast
the duration of the improvement, a reversioner whose
reversion should occur when the improvement had
been exhausted but its cost had not yet been defrayed, would actually be a sufferer to that extent.
But there can be little question that in most, if not
all, cases both these assumptions are incorrect, and
that as a rule improvements made in this way are
either quite permanent or else outlast in a great
measure the duration of the sinking-fund to defray
them. And in general therefore, apart of course from
contract, either the whole of the payments in respect
of the 1*d*. sinking-fund, or so much of these payments
as represents the value of the improvement on the
occurrence of the reversion, is in strict justice
wrongly borne by the building-owner, either directly
or through the medium of the occupier, and should
be borne by the reversioner. It will be observed that
the payments in respect of the 1*d*. sinking-fund form
the *maximum* of the injury inflicted on the building-

owner and of the benefit accruing to the reversioner, and that this maximum may be considerably diminished if and so far as the improvement in question has deteriorated before the occurrence of the reversion.

<small>Only an insignificant part of the rates is therefore in question.</small>

Now, it is matter of common knowledge that the proportion of the rates which is devoted to the service of loans for public improvements is a very small one. To arrive at any exact estimate, in any particular town, would require a far greater knowledge of detail than I can pretend to possess. But in London, where the proportion is supposed to be particularly high, one-fifth of the total rates, or 1s. in the £, would probably be an outside estimate. Of this annual charge of one-fifth of the rates, or 1s. in the £, about three-quarters may probably be taken as the amount required for interest and one-quarter for sinking-fund.* And the result therefore is that, even assuming that all improvements thus made are absolutely permanent, which is very far indeed from being the case, it is only one-twentieth of the rates, or 3d. in the £, which *at the very most* should, in the absence of contract, be charged on the reversioner in relief of the owner. While, making allowance for the actual deterioration of so many improvements, and taking a locality in which there is only an average amount of improvement effected, it would probably be found that not more than from one-thirtieth to one-fiftieth part of the rates should, apart from contract, be charged on the reversioner.

<small>* This is taking the loan throughout the whole period over which the sinking-fund extends. The proportion of the annual charge which is applied to interest is of course largest at first and gradually decreases, while the reverse is the case with the part applied to sinking-fund. But, so far as interest lessens, subsequent building-owners are themselves benefited before the occurrence of the reversion.</small>

The calculations in the preceding paragraph are avowedly rough; but they are probably sufficiently accurate to show that any hardship* suffered in respect of the payment of rates by the building-owner under the 99 years leasehold system is far less than has been generally supposed, and is indeed, even apart from contract, of a comparatively trifling character. It remains to consider what are the practical objections to completely remedying even this trifling grievance by proceeding, in the absence of contract to the contrary, to throw upon reversioners in some shape or form the small proportion of the rates which is employed for their benefit. *[margin: The hardship therefore is in any case very trifling.]*

In the first place it would be necessary to enter into a minute calculation in each case of the amount of the rates levied during the continuance of the lease which has gone to benefit the reversion. This amount will vary not only as between different towns in accordance with the different amounts of the rates and the different proportions of those rates which are expended in permanent or semi-permanent improvements, but also in the same town in accordance with variations in (1) the amounts of the rates from time to time employed in improvements, (2) the comparative durability of the improvements that are effected, and (3) the comparative proximity or remoteness of the reversion. Even on the assumption that the rate for some particular *[margin: Practical objections to change. Minute calculations necessary.]*

---

* I urged in my former work that even this hardship was in fact "much mitigated if not entirely removed" in practice by the fact than an improvement in present value was generally obtained equivalent not only to the interest, but to the sinking-fund in respect of the loan. And I have since found that this view was distinctly put forward by Mr. Tom Taylor, the then Secretary of the Local Government Act Office, in his evidence before Mr. Goschen's Committee on Local Taxation.

improvement is exactly 3*d*. for interest and 1*d*. for sinking-fund over forty years, there would still be enormous difficulties under both of the last two heads. For suppose that the improvement is of such a character that it may be fairly considered to deteriorate 5 per cent. every ten years, and consider at the time when the sinking-fund first begins to run three separate cases : (1) where the reversion is to occur in ten years, (2) where the reversion is to occur in fifty years, and (3) where the reversion is to occur in ninety years. Even in these cases, which have been chosen for the sake of simplicity, it is clear that the benefit done to the reversion would be very different and might be exceedingly difficult to calculate ; and in the far more complex instances which would be perpetually occurring in actual practice the difficulties of mere calculation would be almost insuperable.

Deduction must be deferred. Again, it would be impracticable to deduct rates in respect of reversions while building-leases are still in force and before the reversions have fallen into possession. In many cases peppercorns or other like nominal rents are reserved out of building sites, and there would be no substantial income on which to throw or out of which to deduct rates. Any practical scheme for rating reversions must provide for the burden being thrown on them at the time when they become interests in possession ; but this is only the beginning of a fresh difficulty. Any rates so cast on these reversions when they fall into possession cannot be paid to and retained by the local authorities, since this would be to impose an additional tax on a house in which the interests were divided, in excess of the taxes on a house belonging to an absolute freeholder ; and these rates would accordingly have to be handed back to the persons who had from time to time been the building-owners during the currency of the payment for the improvements in question, unless indeed allowances had been previously made to them during the periods of payment. But to the practical working of either of these plans there are obviously many objections.

Even after all was said and done, and the greatest delay, uncertainty, and friction caused, the result would probably be but a rough measure of justice between the two capitalists—the building-owner and the reversioner. The trouble and expense involved in the ascertainment of the precise allowances to be made, and the consequent uncertainty of income and risk of litigation, would be such as to diminish the value of both these interests in a house. And it would soon prove to be to the advantage both of the landowner and of the builder with whom he deals to avoid this uncertainty and risk by entering into a definite and easily ascertainable arrangement on the subject. *Even so the result would only be rough justice.*

Now, this is exactly what has happened and is happening every day at the present time. The express covenant by the lessee in all building-leases to pay all rates and taxes is a deliberate recognition between the parties of what no doubt the law would otherwise imply, that present burdens should be borne by those in present possession or in present receipt of annual value. But the case is stronger even than this. When the Metropolitan Board of Works was first constituted its only source for raising funds was (in addition to the wine and coal dues) the power to lay under contribution the rateable property in the Metropolis by means of a sewers rate. But Sir John Thwaites, the first chairman of the Board of *It is found convenient to agree to avoid these difficulties.*

Works, in his evidence before the Select Committee of 1866, after stating this, made the following complaint :—

"Our rate is, in point of fact, a sewers rate, and is subject to all the incidents of a sewers rate. That in itself is a landlords' tax, *but it has been the practice for many years for the landlords to dislodge that liability by covenanting with their tenants that the tenants shall pay the sewers rate, and thus casting the charge upon the occupier.*"

<small>Conclusion from this.</small>

Sir John Thwaites himself thought this a great grievance and considered that in practice, though not in theory, landlords did not accept a lower rent in consequence of this liability having been cast on the tenant. But a more natural conclusion would be that it was found inconvenient for one particular rate only to be paid by the landlord, and that therefore *for a fair equivalent* the tenant agreed to pay this rate also.

<small>The agreement is the result of general convenience.</small>

There can indeed be but one inference from these facts. It is impossible to suppose that the invariable insertion of such covenants is the effect of monopoly. It is common knowledge that round London land is in the hands of a vast number of different owners, and that in at least the great majority of instances there is the keenest competition between these owners to attract building to their estates. Any term in building contracts that is considered harsh or unfair must, as a necessary result of this competition, be either modified or abandoned. The invariable presence of a covenant in building-leases that the lessee shall pay all rates and taxes of every kind whatsoever is of itself sufficient proof that lessees do not consider it any real grievance that while they enjoy the property they should discharge all burdens upon it, although some insignificant and scarcely ascertainable part of these burdens may go to improve the reversionary interest of the landowner.

It must always be borne in mind that, as was stated in the last chapter, leases with these covenants are not merely matters of the past, but are being entered into as freely as ever at the present day, with full knowledge of the increase which has taken, and is likely to take, place in the rates on town property. The builder is not generally supposed to be a person unable to take care of himself or who needs an Act of Parliament to protect him. He is compelled to provide for the capitalist who buys from him such an interest in the house built as shall be attractive, or at any rate satisfactory, to his purchaser. One of the terms on which the contract is always entered into is that the lessee shall pay all the rates; and as a matter of contract alone, even if this particular term were an unfair or harsh one, it would be improper to revise it without revising at the same time all the other terms of the contract. But the fact that this particular term is invariably accepted shows that it is considered a fair, reasonable, and convenient term by all the parties concerned. *This is present practice.*

The principle that present interests in property should bear the whole of any present burden is not confined to the rates on leasehold property. A fair analogy is to be found in the case of any kind of property that may be settled so that a life interest is given to one person and a reversionary interest to another *Analogies to this practice.*

The life interest of the tenant for life is perpetually diminishing in value, while concurrently with this decrease the reversionary interest of the reversioner is as continually increasing. And yet during the life of the tenant for life income-tax is levied on his whole income, in spite of the decrease in its capital value and in complete exoneration of the increasing interest of the reversioner. When the reversion falls into possession income-tax will be levied on the full annual income derived from it. But in the case of house property also rates on its full annual value will be borne by the reversionary interest so soon as this becomes an interest in possession.

In the preceding chapter it was objected to the rating of fixed ground-rents not involving a reversion that the effect would be to drive out of investment in houses all cheap or trust capital, and so to raise rents. The same argument seems also to apply to the proposal to rate reversions, at least so far as regards the capital representing the value of sites. Though there would not be the perpetual half-yearly calculation and difficulty, arising from the calculation, proof, and deduction of ever-varying rates, there would be a far more elaborate, difficult, and uncertain adjustment to take place on the occurrence of the reversion. There can be little doubt that the expense, worry, and risk incident to an operation of this kind would operate as a deterrent to the prudent, steady-going investor, who is content with a very moderate return on his capital but requires that return to be made without trouble or anxiety to himself.

In this chapter the reverse method has been adopted to that pursued in the last chapter, and the case principally considered so far has been that of future contracts. As regards existing contracts, little need be added, since the remarks in the last chapter generally apply here also. These contracts have been entered into for good consideration, and by persons well aware of the meaning of the obligations they undertook; and the obligation to pay all rates and taxes is only one of the multifarious terms of the bargain, and cannot therefore be fairly revised alone. But, beyond this, purchases and investments have been made by a most deserving class of investors on the faith of covenants which have only recently been discovered to involve a sort of political immorality. And therefore every consideration of fair-dealing and justice forbids any such tampering with these contracts as is suggested.

A short summary is now appended of the results arrived at in this chapter:— *Summary of conclusions of chapter.*

1. There is, apart from contract, some hardship in the reversion being benefited by the expenditure of rates in permanent or semi-permanent improvements.

2. This hardship falls not on the occupier but on the building-owner. The question is one between two sets of capitalists.

3. The hardship is one of a very trifling nature and applies only to an insignificant proportion of the rates.

4. The hardship could only be rectified by complicated and troublesome calculations and after quite disproportionate worry and expense.

5. It has accordingly been found to be for the general convenience (even where some rates

are expressly thrown on reversions) that building-owners should undertake to pay all the rates, including the small part which benefits reversions.

6. The capitalists who undertake this obligation are a shrewd body of men, quite capable of taking care of themselves.

In particular, as regards future contracts :

7. Cheap or trust capital would be driven out of investment in houses, and rents would be raised, by any enactment casting certain parts of the rates on reversions in spite of contracts to the contrary.

And as regards existing contracts :

8. The rating of reversions would involve the partial confiscation of the property of a most deserving class of investors for the benefit of another class of capitalists.

CHAPTER VIII.

THE RATING OF VACANT BUILDING LAND.

THE question of imposing a special rate on vacant building land in proportion to its capital and not its income value has lately been brought into special prominence by the recommendation to this effect contained in the Report of the Royal Commission on the Housing of the Working Classes. Indeed, it has sometimes been claimed that this recommendation concludes the whole question, and that the only thing now left for consideration is to devise some scheme for giving practical effect to the suggestion. Before adopting such a view, however, it will be only prudent to examine carefully the exact terms of the recommendation, and to ascertain the character and weight of the evidence on which it was based. *The Royal Commission on the Housing of the Working Classes.*

The passage in question runs as follows (pp. 41-2) :—

"Your Majesty's Commissioners must ob- *Recommenda-*
" serve, in reference to Lord Shaftesbury's Acts *tion as to*
" and to nearly every proposal for improving the *vacant building*
" dwellings of the working classes, as well as to *land.*
" other local improvements, that the present inci-
" dence of local taxation stands seriously in the
" way of all progress and reform. They do not feel
" that they are authorised by the terms of Your
" Majesty's Commission to go generally into the

" question of local taxation, but they are of
" opinion that until some reform is introduced
" which shall secure contribution to local expen-
" diture from other sources of income received
" by residents in the locality, in addition to the
" present rateable property, no great progress
" can be made in local improvements.

"In connexion with any such general con-
" sideration of the law of rating attention would
" have to be given to the following facts. At
" present land available for building in the
" neighbourhood of our populous centres,
" though its capital value is very great, is pro-
" bably producing a small yearly return until it
" is let for building. The owners of this land
" are rated not in relation to the real value, but
" to the actual annual income. They can thus
" afford to keep their land out of the market and
" to part with only small quantities, so as to raise
" the price beyond the natural monopoly price
" which the land would command by its advantages
" of position. Meantime the general expenditure
" of the town on improvements is increasing the
" value of their property. If this land were
" rated at, say, 4 per cent. on its selling value,
" the owners would have a more direct incentive
" to part with it to those who are desirous of
" building, and a twofold advantage would
" result to the community. First, all the valu-
" able property would contribute to the rates,
" and thus the burden on the occupiers would be
" diminished by the increase in the rateable pro-
" perty. Secondly, the owners of the building
" land would be forced to offer their land for

"sale, and thus their competition with one
another would bring down the price of building land, and so diminish the tax in the shape
of ground-rent, or price paid for land, which is
now levied on urban enterprise by the adjacent
landowners—a tax, be it remembered, which
is no recompense for any industry or expenditure on their part, but is the natural result of
the industry and activity of the townspeople
themselves. Your Majesty's Commissioners
would recommend that these matters should
be included in legislation when the law of
rating comes to be dealt with by Parliament."

From this view, however, three of the most experienced members of the Commission, Lord Salisbury, Mr. Goschen, and Lord Cross (then Sir Richard Cross), dissented. Lord Salisbury's reasons for this course are succinctly expressed in the following memorandum (p. 61):— *[Dissent of certain members.]*

"A recommendation is made in the Report *[Lord Salisbury's criticism.]*
that vacant land in towns or in the neighbour-
hood of towns should be rated on its capital
instead of its income value. This paragraph
was introduced into the Report just before it
was signed, and I cannot find that it is based
on any evidence laid before the Commission.
I believe that the evil results of such a change
would outweigh its advantages. There may,
possibly, be something to be said for a general
recourse to the American system of taxing
capital instead of income values; but to adopt
it in the isolated case of vacant land in or

"about towns would not only lead to much
"evasion but would have injurious sanitary
"effects. It would operate as a penalty on all
"open spaces except those belonging to a public
"authority. Urban or suburban gardens would
"especially suffer. On the other hand, when
"any pecuniary advantage was to be gained by
"keeping the land vacant, its capital value could
"be easily reduced by collusive alienations of
"portions of it. By a colourable sale of the
"outside edge the capital value of an interior
"block could be, for the time, to a great extent
"destroyed."

Mr. Goschen's and Lord Cross's views.

And Mr. Goschen, with Lord Cross's concurrence, expressed his dissent in the following terms (p. 66):—

" I wish to record my dissent from the re-
"commendation of the Report with reference to
"the rating of vacant land, an extremely im-
"portant point, on which no evidence at all
"proportionate to the magnitude of the subject
"was placed before the Commission.

" The suggestion involves an entirely new
"principle in the law of rating, namely, taxation
"of capital instead of annual value, and I could
"not concur with such a far-reaching change in
"the whole system of local taxation without
"more examination of the bearings of the pro-
"posal than the Commission were able to give
"to them. It is almost certain, too, that if
"vacant land were rated the measure would
"have to be followed by the rating of empty
"houses. Evasion of the law by the running

" up of temporary structures would otherwise
" probably be easy, and there are other con-
" siderations which would also contribute to
" render this further step inevitable. But if that
" were so, the rating of empty houses would act
" as a discouragement of that development of
" building which the rating of vacant land is
" intended to promote, and the general change
" would fail in its purpose."

The above passages have been set out at full length, not only because they contain a useful summary of many of the more important arguments both for and against the proposal to rate vacant building land on its capital value, but also on account of what appears to be their intrinsic authority. The extent of this authority may, however, itself be usefully ascertained before any independent examination is made of these and other arguments on the subject.

There can be no question that in any ordinary case the greatest possible weight would legitimately attach to the Report of so large a majority of the Commission on any subject that was, in fact, before them, and on which they had made full inquiry. The opinion of the majority of a thoroughly competent tribunal on the evidence of witnesses whom they have seen and heard must always be superior in degree to that of persons who can only read a printed record of evidence. But in the present case, startling as it may seem, *there was no evidence at all before the Commission on this point*. No proposal whatever to rate vacant building land was made or discussed by any single witness; and no evidence whatever was given that the present practice is bad, or that an alteration in

The Report has no authority, because it was founded on no evidence.

the law would be advantageous. The opinion expressed on this subject in the Report must, therefore, be regarded as the casually expressed opinion of a certain number of gentlemen with no extraordinary means of information on the subject, not as a judicial or authoritative *conclusion*—for, indeed, there were no materials whatever from which a conclusion could be drawn. On this point the Report of the Royal Commission carries no authority whatever. The matter is still *res integra*, and must be considered on its merits.

<small>Summary of the reasons for a change.</small>
It will have been noted that both in the Report of the Royal Commission, and in the article in the *Westminster Review* before cited, and in Mr. Sidney Webb's pamphlet, there are three main reasons given for rating vacant building land, namely: first, that such building land is benefited by the expenditure of the rates*; secondly, that the effect of rating vacant building land would be to prevent its being held off the building market; and thirdly, that the area of local taxation would in this manner be widened. And the evidence of Mr. Cooper, Mr. Fatkin, Mr. Mackenzie, Mr. Rhodes, and Mr. Saunders, who were the principal witnesses who gave evidence in favour of the proposal in question before the Select Committee on Town Holdings, was, roughly speaking, based on the same arguments, aggravated to some extent by a consideration of the great increase of capital value which had in some instances accrued to

---

* The Report of the Royal Commission speaks only of this land being benefited by the general " expenditure of the town on *improvements*," which, as we have seen, absorb but a very small part of the rates; but as it goes on to recommend rating to the *whole* rates, it must for the sake of consistency be supposed to mean to include in the term " *improvements* " the whole expenditure of the rates.

individual landowners. But of these three arguments the second, and still more the third, are arguments merely of *expediency*, not of *justice*; and accordingly, though not destitute of some force, carry nothing like the same weight as the first, and may be briefly dealt with at once. The mere fact that the area of local taxation will be widened can be no reason or justification for including within it property which is not concerned with or benefited by local taxation. And it is of no use to endeavour to give a further impetus to vacant building land being brought into the market * when the general tendency of landowners already is to anticipate, rather than to defer, the moment for letting their land for building. Such legislation, if it should not result in colourable evasions, would at any rate have a tendency to develop and encourage the "jerry" builder to a most unfortunate extent. Few spectacles, indeed, can be more melancholy than that, which is so often exhibited, of an estate forced prematurely into the building market, and half-covered with dismal erections, of which many are unfinished and more unoccupied.

Ryde (1886), 2,942. Garrard (1887), 4,966. Wallis (1888), 2,942.

On the other hand, the first reason above stated is one of *justice*, and therefore of the utmost weight. If vacant building land is in fact benefited by the expenditure of the rates of the town which it adjoins, it seems only just (unless there are overwhelming reasons to the contrary) that it should

The reason from resulting benefit is the strong one.

* Indeed, the result would more probably be to crush out the small holder of vacant building land, who could not afford to pay rates without receiving income. Any reader of Mr. Henry George's *Progress and Poverty* will not be inclined to think that the plan which is prevalent in America of taxing land (and all other property) on *capital* value has prevented land being held back in that country from the building market or by speculators.

Garrard (1887), 5,032 *et seq.*

contribute to the rates from which it derives benefit. If, on the other hand, vacant building land is *not* benefited by the expenditure of these rates, it seems equally clear that it should *not* so contribute. It is necessary here again to consider, at any rate in some rough measure, the purposes to which the rates levied in towns are devoted.

Vacant building land is not intentionally or immediately benefited by the rates.

Immediately that the question is regarded from this point of view, the first point that will probably strike the student of the subject is that if vacant building land *does* derive benefit from the rates, such a result is entirely foreign to the intention of those who administer the expenditure of the rates. This administration is, as I understand it, directed towards providing certain necessaries and comforts of life for the individuals forming the community who inhabit the area from which the rates are levied. And if any other purpose should animate the local authorities in their expenditure, there can be no question that they would soon be called to account by those whose money they are expending. Nor can there be much doubt that the local authorities do not in fact expend the produce of the rates for the benefit of vacant building land. Vacant building land does not house any community requiring the lighting or repair of streets or the maintenance of sewers, the payment of a police force, the provision of education, the support of the poor, or the satisfaction of the other multifarious needs which are met out of rates and absorb the great bulk of them. The vacant building land which surrounds a town adds no more to the expenditure of that town than a similar amount of land a hundred miles off. The rates of a town, or the vast proportion of them, are devoted to the purposes of that town as it exists, and of the community inhabiting it for the time being. So soon as the vacant building land ceases to be vacant and is covered and inhabited, it will both contribute to the rates and share in the benefit of their expenditure; but till that time arrives it does not contribute to the rates because it is not benefited by them.

It is indeed sometimes said that, although rates may not actually be expended in supplying any needs of adjacent building land, it is the expenditure of the rates of the town population which causes the increase in the value of the building land, and that therefore it is only fair to charge a part of that expenditure on the land in question. But this argument will not bear careful examination. The growth of the population and the expansion of the town, which are themselves due in nineteen cases out of twenty to natural advantages of position, are the cause of a demand for building land in the vicinity; and not the expenditure of the rates at all. If the population of a town is stationary or declining, however great the expenditure of the rates may be, there will be no great demand for, or increase in the price of, adjacent building land; while on the other hand, if the population of a town is increasing fast there will be a great competition for building land on the outskirts and a great increase in its value however low the rates in the town may be. Indeed, so far from high rates benefiting building land, it is well known that they act as a positive check on its development, for reasons which have been set out in a previous part of this work.

The growth of towns and the expenditure of rates are quite different causes.

To deal completely with the subject, however, it is still necessary to consider that small proportion of

The proportion of rates spent on improvements.

the rates which is expended in permanent improvements, or rather that still more insignificant part of that proportion which goes to defray the sinking-fund in respect of those improvements. For though the general expenditure of the rates is not intended to, and does not in fact, benefit vacant building land, it may yet be that, as in the case of reversions, monies spent in discharging the *capital* cost of permanent improvements are in fact a benefit to vacant building land, and should therefore to that extent be defrayed or contributed to by a special tax upon such land. This is indeed, as has already been pointed out, the apparent meaning of one of the reasons for rating vacant building land given in the Report of the Royal Commission on the Housing of the Working Classes, though the recommendation which is there made goes very far beyond the reason, and applies to the whole rates, not to the very small proportion of them now being considered.

This question is hardly of practical importance.

The answer to the question mooted in the last paragraph is rather a practical than a theoretical one. It will be remembered that streets and sewers for the accommodation of vacant building land as and when it is brought into the market for building are constructed at the expense of the landowner, not of the local authority ; so that these works, which are often regarded by the general public as improvements effected at the public expense, are not really in question at all. And the public improvements which are in fact effected at the public expense are not so effected for the benefit of the vacant building land surrounding a town, but for the benefit of the town itself; are not as a rule undertaken on the outskirts of the town but in central positions ; and benefit the outlying building land (which of course forms the vast bulk of vacant building land) if at all, to a very small extent in comparison with the more central districts. Now and again such a work as a public park may be created at the general expense in some comparatively remote district of London. But even in these cases the surrounding district is generally densely crowded, and any large quantity of vacant building land is not within range; indeed, it is matter of everyday observation that where there is much vacant building land it is itself turned to many of the purposes of a public park or playground.

The position of vacant building land in these respects was clearly put before the Select Committee by Mr. Wallis, the agent of the Eastbourne estates of the Duke of Devonshire, which are, as is well known, being developed on a system of leases with an option to the lessee to purchase the freehold. Such vacant building land does not, he said, "impose any addi- "tional works by the fact of its lying fallow on "the part of the corporate body. . . . *The rate-* "*payers are not paying anything in respect of it.* These "people, as far as my experience goes (and it is "rather large*), *are not in advance of their works in* "*anticipation of certain buildings.* We have generally "to push a corporation forward." This answer obviously includes both the question of the ordinary annual expenditure of the rates and that of any extraordinary expenditure on permanent improvements. The latter expenditure, which is, as has been seen, the only one in respect of which any claim could legitimately be made against vacant building land, is not made for the purpose of benefiting vacant building land, and does not in fact benefit it except in rare

Improvements are not made for vacant building land.

Wallis (1888), 2,785. And see Garrard (1887), 4,969.

* Mr. Wallis was the first Mayor of Eastbourne.

instances or to an exceedingly limited extent. In very special cases, a rate for some special improvement obviously for the benefit of a vacant area might, on proof of the facts to the satisfaction of Parliament, be authorised to be levied on that area. But there is no case for charging on vacant building land *generally* any part of the rates of the adjacent town on account of any substantial benefit accruing to such land through the expenditure of the rates.

Further reasons against the change must be stated.

The reasons given in the preceding paragraphs against the proposals to rate vacant building land will probably be considered a sufficient answer to the arguments previously stated in favour of those proposals. But the case in favour of the present system and against any such change would be extremely incomplete without noticing some additional reasons of considerable weight and interest.

Difficulty of defining vacant building land.

The difficulty of defining what is vacant building land is an objection rather to the practical working out of the proposal in question than to the theoretical arguments in favour of it, but still there can be no doubt that this difficulty would be extremely great. Mr. Garrard, a surveyor of great experience, in his evidence before the Select Committee on Town Holdings, said : " I defy anyone to say when " land is building land. It grows imperceptibly " into building land." And whatever rough practical definition of building land were adopted, not only would all sorts of evasions be resorted to for the purpose of eluding the definition, but the grossest anomalies would be produced. Land actually fenced in and occupied for agricultural, accommodation, or market-gardening purposes could hardly be brought within the definition ; while unfenced land through

Garrard (1887), 5,036.

which a road had been driven by the landowner would almost certainly be included. Yet any benefit arising from the growth of the town or the expenditure of the rates would increase the value of a piece of land in the former condition as much as if it were in the latter condition. And, besides the anomaly arising from this fact, the tendency would be for landowners to keep back the construction of roads and the development of their land as much as possible till actual building took place, and so not only to retard development, but ultimately to develop in a piecemeal, and therefore in a more expensive and less satisfactory, manner.

Again, the effect of such a measure has to be considered with regard to the comparatively small amounts of vacant building land that are kept open in the middle of towns as parks, gardens, or open spaces of a private or semi-private nature. Amongst such spaces in London are included the gardens of the Archbishop's palace at Lambeth and of the Inns of Court, the ornamental gardens in the centres of the larger squares, and the parks and gardens attached to private houses, of which, perhaps, the park of Holland House may be selected as the most striking example. There can be no question of the expediency of preserving these additional breathing spaces or "lungs," or of the undesirability of adding additional piles of bricks and mortar within the present already overburdened area. And it is hardly too much to say that a sigh of relief passed through Western London when a contradiction was recently given to a rumour that the park of Holland House was to be handed over to the speculative builder. Yet the first result of rating vacant land on its

Effect on open spaces in towns of rating on capital value.

capital value if devoted to building purposes would be to drive into the building market all, or most, of the private or semi-private open spaces already existing in towns, and to prevent the reservation of any such open spaces in all schemes for the development of building land in the future.

<small>Such rating is in conflict with the principles of English taxation.</small>
But perhaps the strongest of all the reasons against rating vacant building land on its capital value has still to be stated. It is that such rating is in conflict with the principles of taxation which are at present accepted in this country, and could only fairly be adopted as part of a general and sweeping change. At the present time, and in this country, so far as taxation is based on property at all, it is estimated on the income resulting from property and not on its capital value. And it would therefore be obviously unfair in the case of one particular class of property to reverse this process, and to tax on capital and not on income. Nor indeed, strange as it may appear to those numerous advocates of change who are always ready to assume that any system prevailing in this benighted island is incomparably inferior to that adopted in any foreign country, is this method of taxing income instead of capital an entirely unreasonable one. Let us briefly examine a few of its more important advantages.

<small>Adam Smith's principles of taxation.</small>
Of the four great principles of taxation enunciated by Adam Smith and substantially concurred in by subsequent writers,* at least the first three, and probably to some extent the fourth also, are in favour of taxing income rather than capital. The material

---

* See Mill, *Principles of Political Economy*, Book V. chap. ii. § 1. (pp. 483-4, People's Edition, 1865), from which the quotation of Adam Smith's principles is taken.

parts of these principles for the present purpose are as follows, the italics being mine :—

"1. The subjects of every State ought to "contribute to the support of the government "as nearly as possible in proportion to their "respective abilities: that is, in proportion to "the *revenue* which they respectively enjoy "under the protection of the State. . . .

"2. The tax which each individual is bound "to pay ought to be certain, and not arbitrary. "The time of payment, the manner of payment, "the quantity to be paid, ought all to be plain "and clear to the contributor and to every other "person. Where it is otherwise, every person "subject to the tax is more or less in the power of "the tax-gatherer . . . . The certainty of what "each individual ought to pay is, in taxation, a "matter of so great importance that *a very consi-* "*derable degree of inequality, it appears, I believe*, "*from the experience of all nations, is not near so* "*great an evil as a small degree of uncertainty.*

"3. Every tax ought to be levied at the "time or in the manner in which it is most "likely to be convenient for the contributor to "pay it. *A tax upon the rent of land or of houses* "*payable at the same term at which such rents are* "*usually paid* is levied at a time when it is most "likely to be convenient for the contributor to "pay. . . .

"4. Every tax ought to be so contrived as "both to take out and to keep out of the pockets "of the people as little as possible over and "above what it brings into the public treasury

And see Mathews (1888), 1,410 *et seq.*

"of the State. .... First, *the levying of it may require a great number of officers*. ...."

<small>Application of these axioms.</small> It is hardly necessary to point out the applicability of these four classical axioms to the matter now in question. By the first *revenue* and not capital value is distinctly put forward as the basis of taxation. In regard to the second it is obvious that, whatever the degree of certainty that may be attained with regard to the capital value of land, as to which there is some dispute, there can be no question but that there is a much greater degree of certainty as to the income derived from it. The third axiom is so precisely in point as to require no comment; and as to the last, a larger and more experienced and trustworthy (and therefore more highly paid) staff will necessarily be required for purposes of valuation if this is to be made on the footing of a hypothetical capital value, and not of a comparatively certain income value. The teaching of the above passage could hardly be more decidedly against the proposal to rate vacant building land on its capital value.

<small>The community can hardly do better than to allow individuals to follow their own profit, and to rate them on the result.</small> It is indeed often said that individuals designedly keep land back from the market to profit by the enhanced value that will accrue to it. If there were an enhanced value thus to be gained which was actually produced by the expenditure of the money of other people, not only would this be an illegitimate method to adopt, but such a practice might be so tempting as to become comparatively common. But it has been seen that this inducement does not exist. And a complete practical answer to any argument of this kind seems to me that the owners of land, as of every other kind of property, must live on income and

not on capital; that even if a man abstains for the moment from securing an immediate income from property, it is with a view of obtaining an ultimate income from the same source which shall be so much larger as to fully compensate him for his abstention; and that if the community are entitled to a percentage on the property of an individual, they can hardly do better than to allow him to develop his property in the way that appears most advantageous to himself, and then take their percentage on that result. The community will lose with the individual by any present sacrifice of income; but they will proportionally gain by that ultimate increase of income, the prospect of which has induced him to make the present sacrifice. And they will therefore do wisely by permitting individuals to consult their own pecuniary interest and by then taking toll of the result.

That in accordance with the above principles income and not capital value has in fact been adopted as the measure of taxation in this country needs but little proof. Great engineering works like the Severn Tunnel or the Forth Bridge, which take years to complete, have of course an enormous capital value long before they are in a position to earn revenue; yet until this happens they are unrated. Collections of old china or of pictures have a large and (if well selected) a growing capital value, yet no rates are levied on them. The reversion to property in settlement may be of enormous value, and grows in value as the tenant for life ages or becomes infirm or sickly; and yet income-tax is thrown exclusively on the present income of the tenant for life, the capital value of which is steadily declining. In none of

Instances of capital value being unrated.

these cases is capital value regarded as a proper subject for taxation.

[sidenote: Are American methods to be followed?] There is still one possible alternative, namely, that we should throw over the canons of taxation at present prevailing in this country, and, so far as we impose any direct tax on property at all, tax vacant building land and all other property whatever on the basis of capital value and not of income value. In this respect indeed the States of the American Union are often held up to us as an example; but before adopting such a course it may be well to learn what Americans themselves think of this system. It may be remembered that in a previous chapter a passage was given from a speech of Mr. Goschen in the year 1871 in which he quoted an opinion of an American authority, Mr. Wells, as to the iniquities perpetrated under the American system, and the superiority of our own rating system. But quite recently an elaborate account * of the system in America has been given by Professor Ely, who as a Professor of Political Economy in the Johns Hopkins University, Baltimore, and a member of the Maryland Tax Commission, appears to possess a singular combination of theoretical and practical knowledge of the subject. *[sidenote: No. For they lead to fraud and unfairness.]* It is impossible within the limits of the present treatise to give any account of the contents of this thoughtful and practical work. But nothing could be stronger than the denunciation which it contains of the universal fraud and roguery which is produced by the system of taxing real and personal property on their capital value, or than the impression which it creates in favour of a system of taxation based in general on income and not on capital.

* *Taxation in American States and Cities.* New York: Thomas Y. Crowell & Co.

The following is again a summary of the more important conclusions arrived at in this chapter:— *Summary of conclusions of chapter.*

1. The report of the majority of the Royal Commission on the Housing of the Working Classes in favour of rating vacant building land *is based on no evidence whatever, and therefore is not authoritative.*

2. To rate vacant building land would result in throwing it more into the hands of the rich.

3. Vacant building land should not be rated because it does not cause, and is not in general benefited by, the expenditure of the rates.

4. It would be difficult to define building land, and both difficult and expensive to ascertain its value.

5. For the last two reasons, and because the tax would be on capital and not on income, such a tax would offend against sound principle.

6. Such a tax is in conflict with the principles which govern the taxation of other property in this country. An alteration should be made with regard to all property, or else with regard to none.

7. The taxation of capital value in America results in great abuses and oppression and is far inferior to our system of taxing income.

CHAPTER IX.

GENERAL REMARKS AND CONCLUSION.

A few points still to be noticed.

THERE is no need to make any formal summary in this chapter of the conclusions that have been arrived at in opposition to all current proposals to tax ground-rents or ground-values. The short summaries at the end of the preceding chapters will sufficiently serve this purpose. But there are one or two points that have been already touched, which are nevertheless of such importance as to justify some amount of repetition and enforcement. It is to this purpose that this short final chapter will be devoted.

The question is an owners' not an occupiers' question.

It has been already sufficiently pointed out that the current proposals for a change in rating are not of real importance as between occupiers and "building-owners," but as between "building-owners" and the owners of fixed rents and reversions. In the former case not only do the owners already pay the whole rates in the great majority of town holdings, but the shortness of most occupation tenancies, the competition which prevails between different kinds of tenancy, and the facilities for changing residences, all tend to prevent any increase in rates being unduly thrown on the occupier.* And so the question, in fact, comes to be one between two sets of capitalists who divide up between them the value of town houses, namely,

---

* Even where the question is professedly treated as one between owner and occupier it generally slides unconsciously into a question

the building-owner on the one side and the owner of the fixed rent-charge, or ground-rent, on the other side. And between these two persons there seem to me to be three broad aspects in which the case may be considered. They are these:—(1) How, independently of any covenant to pay rates, ought the rates to be adjusted between these two persons? (2) Is there any sufficient reason for prohibiting, by legislation, the covenant which is always entered into that the building-owner shall pay the rates? And (3): Is there any sufficient reason for setting aside existing covenants that the building-owner shall pay the rates? A few paragraphs will be devoted to answering each of these important questions. *Three broad aspects.*

It has been seen that where land is let for building purposes at a rent-charge or rent instead of being sold outright, the bargain is that the landowner shall receive not a certain proportion of the rents and *A rent-charger has an interest in but not any ownership of a house.*

between two sets of owners, as the following curious passage from Lord Hobhouse's article in the *Contemporary Review* will show. The italics are mine:—

"In the case of *old* leases the owner's property has been "improved by the forced payments *of the occupier* under new "laws and a new policy which could not have entered into the "calculations of the parties. I will give as an example the lease "under which I hold my house. It was made *in 1833*, and "it contains the usual covenant to pay all rates and taxes . . . "*As assignee* I have undertaken to perform that contract" (p. 155).

An *occupation* lease granted in the year 1833, and in full swing in 1888! At any rate this is hardly a typical case. But there can be little doubt that the lease in question was in fact an *ownership* lease, for which money was paid, and that it is as an owner and *purchaser* of the lease, not as an occupier, that Lord Hobhouse is (or rather might have been) prejudiced. If, instead of *purchasing* from his predecessor in title, he had taken an occupation lease from him, the covenant as occupier to pay all rates and taxes would have been to pay the rates and taxes now existing.

profits of the building, but a fixed sum which shall participate neither in any increase nor in any decrease. And therefore, though the owner of this fixed annual payment has an *interest* in the house, he is not the *owner* of any part of it. He is in precisely the position of an annuitant, mortgagee, or other incumbrancer entitled to a fixed sum out of the income of the house, but not entitled to any share in the profits or increase of it, all of which will be taken by the " building-owner." Since then he does not share in the advantages, he should also be relieved from any share in the burdens of ownership. The difference between a person so entitled to a fixed annual payment and a person entitled to an aliquot share of profits is, to my mind, precise and definite and exactly equivalent to the difference between a man who is a creditor or incumbrancer of a partnership and a member of the firm. And equally precise and definite is the analogy between the man entitled to this fixed annual payment and a mortgagee, who is indeed always interested in his security being *maintained* at a level sufficient to secure his debt, but can never share in any value that may be added to it, and is not therefore expected to share in any of the burdens cast on it.

<small>Popular phraseology misleading.</small> This state of facts appears often to be obscured by the popular phraseology (from which I cannot profess to have shaken myself free even in the present treatise) which speaks of the one man as the owner of the land and the other as the owner of the building. No doubt originally the one man *was* the owner of the land, and the other, by himself or those who financed him, found the money to erect the building. But on the conclusion of this opera-

tion the land and the building become one, and the ownership of each part is divided in precisely the same manner and to precisely the same extent. The man who was the owner of the land has become merely the owner of a fixed rent-charge or ground-rent issuing out of ground and building alike. The man who built the house or the purchaser from him has become the owner both of the building and of the land, subject only to a fixed rent-charge or ground-rent.

The importance of a clear grasp of this central fact can hardly be overestimated. In the popular mind the man who *was* the landowner *is* the landowner still, and anything which, like the expenditure of the rates, may be supposed to enhance the value of the land is supposed to enure to the benefit of this landowner. Indeed, the whole basis of the argument in many writings, and in Mr. Moulton's pamphlet in particular, appears to rest on the assumption that " swollen " land-values go into the pockets of those who are receiving the fixed primary rents, which are either original ground-rents or have been brought by the increase of ground-value within the rent which the ground would now fetch if vacant. But in truth the exact contrary is the case. All increase of ground-value (that is, of the income value of land) belongs to the persons who *have* the land in their possession—that is, to the persons who have the buildings and the land to let at a rack-rent to occupiers or to enjoy themselves. The persons who have the buildings and land together to dispose of and turn to account are the landowners in the proper sense of the word, though their land has buildings on it. The persons who receive the rents representing the

The owner-ship of land and house is identical.

former value of the land have *ceased* to be the landowners, have therefore ceased to be benefited by the increase in the value of the land, and have also rightly ceased to be burdened with the charges on the land.

<small>The question of a reversion considered.</small> So far, then, as the interest of landowners may have been reduced to mere fixed rent-charges or ground-rents, or so far as other persons may have acquired such an interest in land covered with buildings, natural justice would, apart altogether from contract, prescribe that they should be indemnified from any burdens in respect of the land and buildings. But so far as any such person may, in addition to his present fixed ground-rent, have a tangible reversion in the land and buildings (a point not hitherto considered in this chapter), natural justice would also prescribe, apart from contract, that he should in some way or other contribute to that part of these burdens which, as representing permanent improvements, will enure to the benefit of his reversion when it falls in. It has been seen, however, that this part of these burdens is comparatively insignificant and very difficult to calculate; and that while these reasons might of themselves, as in other analogous cases, be sufficient to justify this part of the burdens also being defrayed by the landowner in receipt of the profits for the time being, it is at any rate a natural, legitimate, and convenient thing that a contract should be entered into that this should be done.

<small>The ordinary contract as to rates is a proper and reasonable arrangement.</small> This consideration, indeed, helps to furnish an answer to the second of the three questions above stated, namely, whether there is any sufficient reason for prohibiting a covenant that a building-lessee should pay all rates. Where there is no reversion or no practical reversion attaching to the interest

of the owner of the fixed rent-charge or groundrent, it has been seen that such a covenant is but the solemn, verbal recognition of an obligation that should in any case attach to the estate of the man who is the real owner of land and buildings alike. And where there is a practical reversion such a covenant only expresses a natural and legitimate arrangement on the part of both parties that the person who should in any case bear the vast proportion of the rates, and could in any event be justly relieved only of an amount of these rates both insignificant and excessively troublesome to ascertain, should also undertake the settlement of this trifling and almost unascertainable portion. Why in the world should legislation be invoked to prohibit an agreement founded on such purely practical and businesslike grounds?

But a few more words are necessary to press fully home the true force of this argument. The contracts that are every day made between landowners and builders are fully considered and threshed out between the parties in every possible debateable item. The exact amount of ground-rent, the value of the houses to be built, the length of time for which a peppercorn rent is to run, the exact covenants to be inserted in the lease— these are but a few of the terms which are exhaustively debated between the parties, assisted almost always by solicitors and sometimes also by counsel. And as a result of these discussions modifications of all kinds are from time to time adopted in all these particulars. The covenant by the lessee to pay all rates and taxes is, so far as my experience goes, *never contested at all and invariably inserted.* What other reason for this can be given than that between business men it is recognised that the man who has

[sidenote: Its universality is the best proof of its convenience.]

the small fixed income should get it net, and that the man who has the bulk of the present income and the whole of any increase should bear all burdens, even if some small part of them should ultimately enure to the benefit of the other party?

Why should such contracts be interfered with in the case of houses alone?

But the matter does not end even here. Such arrangements are constantly entered into with regard to many other kinds of property. All mortgagees receive a limited but unburdened income, while all mortgagors take the whole of any benefit that may accrue and bear the whole of any burden. The same is the case between the holders of the debenture and preference stocks of railways, canals, waterworks, gasworks, docks, and almost every other important undertaking on the one hand and the holders of the ordinary stock and shares in the same concerns on the other hand. Nay, the pressing need at the present day for investments which return a small but fairly certain income is still further illustrated by the success which has attended the recent " stock-"splitting" operations of trust investment and conversion companies, and by the proposals which are at present being brought forward for legislative sanction to similar proceedings in the case of the ordinary stocks of the more prosperous railway companies. Is it to be said that house property is the only form of investment out of which investors are to be prohibited from securing to themselves a small but invariable return ? And are legislators prepared to drive out of house property the whole of the supply of cheap or trust capital ? This would inevitably be the result of any such legislation, and would necessarily cause (as has been previously shown) a rise in house-rent. It must require a much stronger case than any that has yet been put forward to cause the legislature to take so disastrous a step as this.

Some evidence that was given before the Select Committee on Town Holdings is particularly apposite to this part of the subject. It was stated that builders having freehold land to develop and traders owning the freehold of their premises often raise capital cheaply by converting themselves into lessees and selling to a purchaser the freehold of their property subject to a lease to themselves. And this plan is said to be preferable to raising the amount required on mortgage, because there is no liability to have a principal sum called in. It is clear that if the income to be offered to a purchaser on such a transaction should be necessarily a fluctuating one, any money raised in this way would be obtained on terms so much more onerous that the method would probably have to be abandoned altogether. Yet what is there unsound or improper in such a transaction as this? And what necessity has been shown for any legislative interference as between two sets of capitalists who so thoroughly understand their own business? *An example.* Tewson (1887), 2,925-2,928. Garrard (1887), 4,926. Vigers (1887), 1,534.

Assume for the moment that the freeholder so wishing to raise funds was a company, and that the company was proposing to raise £25,000 by selling a freehold rent-charge of £1,000 a year on property of the annual value of £5,000 per annum. According to the new views this £1,000 a year must, in all future cases at least, be subjected to a proportionate share of the rates on the property. And yet the company can obtain substantially the same result by creating perpetual debentures carrying £1,000 per annum interest and secured on the pro- *Another example.*

perty in question, and the interest on these debentures will admittedly not be rateable. Where is the difference in principle between the two methods which should cause this startling difference in result?

Existing contracts. The negative answers that have been given to the first two of the three questions that were propounded above for solution necessarily involve a negative answer to the proposal to set aside existing contracts to pay all rates. If such contracts are in accordance with natural justice, and if there is no sufficient reason for prohibiting them in the future, it would *a fortiori* be improper to set aside *existing* contracts of this kind. But the argument for *supporting* existing contracts is a cumulative one, and it is but right to set out those additional reasons which, even if such contracts went beyond the natural justice of the case independently of contract, and ought to be restrained in the future, would still appear sufficient to prohibit any interference with existing contracts.

The strength of these contracts; The covenant to pay all rates and taxes which is contained in a building-lease is a bargain entered into upon good consideration and by a perfectly competent party; and above all it is one part, and one part only, of a much more varied and extensive contract. On what principle is such a bargain to be reopened at all? And if reopened, why is not the whole contract to be reopened at the same time? Freeholders who have let at a small fixed rent *because* it is fixed and *because* it is to be kept free from the payment of rates and taxes, will certainly not suffer on the whole if, while they are deprived of the benefit of this indemnity on the one hand, they are on the other allowed to reap the benefit of the increase of land-value which has since occurred; but will lessees and other " building-owners " view the matter in the same light? Is not their demand merely to have the contract reopened only as to that item of it which is to their disadvantage? And is this a demand which either justice or common sense can recommend?

But the case is even stronger than if it rested between the original parties to the contract. Where the building contract is an old one—and it is these instances that are said to be particularly deserving of relief—there have in general been several changes of the ownership in each interest in the house. In these cases the purchaser of the interest of the building-owner has in each case purchased with full knowledge of the obligation to pay all rates and taxes, and has adjusted the terms of his purchase accordingly; while the purchaser of the fixed rent-charge or ground-rent has also been aware of the indemnity against rates to which his interest is entitled, and has given a higher price in consequence. On what principle is the former to be relieved of a part of the obligation subject to which he purchased, and the latter to be mulcted of a part of the indemnity for which he has paid? Why is Peter to be robbed to pay Paul? Or, as a writer in the *Star* of the 5th November, 1888, trenchantly expressed it:— *particularly as between subsequent investors.*

" For my part I don't see the fun of taxing
" the Duke of Westminster simply to put money
" into the pockets of the trustees of the Cubitt
" estate in Pimlico, or taxing the Marquis of
" Salisbury to enrich the leaseholders of his
" slum property."

It has indeed been urged that the proposed tax on ground-rents will be of the nature of a new tax, *Examination of some argu-*

ments for breaking such contracts.

which the State has always a right to impose; and the analogy of income-tax is also sometimes invoked. Neither argument, however, will bear examination. Apart from the fact that the covenant contained in building contracts does in fact extend to new taxes, it is clear that the tax would not in fact be a new one at all, but merely a method of enabling one set of capitalists to throw on another set part of the burden of an existing tax. And this marks the distinction between such a tax as is proposed and income-tax. Not only is income-tax thrown on every class of income alike, but the person who deducts income-tax on any payment of rent does so *only for the purpose of handing it over to the State, not so as to retain the deduction for his own benefit.* The contract between the parties is no more altered than if the rent were still paid in full, and the income-tax were then paid by the receiver of rent out of the income received. The deduction is merely a method of collection for revenue purposes. But the very object of the present proposals is to relieve the person making the deduction and to allow him to retain the deduction for himself. No further revenue whatever would accrue to the local authority or other body receiving the tax. The result would be, not that any new tax would be paid, but that one interest in land would directly contribute to taxation *in exoneration of another interest.*

Even a new tax may amount to confiscation.

But even if the tax proposed *were* a new one, that would not justify the imposition on one particular existing class of property of a heavy burden unbalanced by any counterbalancing burden on other kinds of property. Mr. Mathews has well pointed out in a note to his evidence before the Select Committee

Mathews (1888), 1,668.

on Town Holdings that to a proposal of this character applies with equal justice the language of John Stuart Mill respecting "the proposition of an "exclusive tax on realised property." The quotation is as follows* :—

> " Except the proposal of applying a sponge
> " to the national debt, no such palpable violation
> " of common honesty has found sufficient
> " support in this country during the present
> " generation to be regarded as within the
> " domain of discussion. . . . .
> " The burthen thus exclusively thrown on
> " the owners of the smaller portion of the wealth
> " of the community would not even be a
> " burthen on that *class* of persons in perpetual
> " succession, but would fall exclusively on those
> " who happened to compose it when the tax was
> " laid on. As land and those particular securities
> " would thenceforth yield a smaller net income
> " relatively to the general interest of capital and
> " to the profits of trade; the balance would rectify
> " itself by a permanent depreciation of those
> " kinds of property. Future buyers would
> " acquire land and securities at a reduction of
> " price equivalent to the peculiar tax, which
> " tax they would, therefore, escape from paying;
> " while the original possessors would remain
> " burthened with it even after parting with the
> " property, since they would have sold their
> " land or securities at a loss of value equivalent
> " to the fee-simple of the tax. Its imposition

* *Principles of Political Economy*, Book V., chap. 2, § iii. (People's Edition, p. 487).

" would thus be tantamount to the confiscation
" for public uses of a percentage of their pro-
" perty equal to the percentage laid on their
" income by the tax. That such a proposition
" should find any favour is a striking instance
" of the want of conscience in matters of
" taxation resulting from the absence of any
" fixed principles in the public mind, and of any
" indication of a sense of justice on the subject
" in the general conduct of governments.
" Should the scheme ever enlist a large party
" in its support, the fact would indicate a laxity
" of pecuniary integrity in national affairs
" scarcely inferior to American repudiation."

With this quotation the present treatise may fitly close. There can be no fear of the proposals to rate ground-rents being adopted, as to existing contracts at any rate, if our politics are still animated by a tithe of the sterling honesty and independence of thought which breathe through every line of this passage.

APPENDIX.

(See pages 67 and 68.)

THE central point of my examination of Mr. Moulton's proposal and of his reply consists in an illustration which he had given in his pamphlet and which I adopted with a slight modification. It is as follows :—

A, a landowner, has leased a site for its full value, £100 per annum, to B, a builder, who has erected thereon a house worth £600 a year (*i.e.*, £500 in addition to the original ground-value of £100), and has secured his profit by letting the house to C (*alias* Bb), in consideration of a premium, for the whole term at £500 per annum. The land is then supposed to increase in value to £500 per annum, and therefore the house and land to £1,000 per annum, the whole increase of £400 per annum thus going into the pocket of C.

Under Mr. Moulton's scheme I apprehended that after this increase of ground-value B's *fixed* net rent of £400 per annum would now be rated to its full extent as having fallen within the limit of ground-value, *while every penny of the increase of £400 per annum would go unrated into the pocket of C.* The result is both startling and ludicrous, and sufficient of itself to condemn any scheme which should bring it about; and yet Mr. Moulton acknowledges that this *is* the result which his proposal would produce, and appears to see no absurdity in it. And his only answer consists in exclaiming "Does not B share in the rise of " ground-value?" and in pointing out that the *capital* value of B's rent will have increased, as he estimates, from 18 years' purchase to 27 years' purchase.*

But this importation of *capital* value into the discussion is in fact entirely foreign to the whole spirit of Mr. Moulton's pamphlet, which deals with income and income alone. Nay, the very phrase "ground-value," from which he seeks to extract suggestions of capital value, has been several times defined by him in his pamphlet, once even in italics, as the *actual rental value of the land*, and was quoted (also in italics) in the summary which I gave of his pamphlet before criticising it.

As an *argumentum ad hominem* this would probably be accepted as conclusive; but the matter is too important to be concluded by a mere triumph over an adversary. Assume, for the moment, that capital value and not merely income value ought to be taken into account. Is it satisfactory that the whole burden of the rates on £400 a year should be thrown on B because the capital value of his investment has increased by a few years' purchase, while C, *whose income and capital have both been increased £400 per cent.*, escapes entirely scot-free? And will it still be satisfactory (as would undoubtedly be the case under Mr. Moulton's proposals) that B's £400 per annum should still bear this burden without diminution, even when it approaches—for it is only a terminable annuity—within twenty, or ten, or two years of its termination and so is losing all its capital value?

But the subject may be looked at from another point of view. The value of buildings bears no necessary or fixed relation to the ground-rents of the sites on which they are erected; and we may well suppose, without altering the

---

* Twenty-seven years' purchase for this improved *leasehold* ground-rent is a ridiculous valuation to be made by a professing expert. Mr. Edward Tewson, the well-known estate-agent, has been kind enough to value at my request this hypothetical ground-rent. He values it *before* the rise in ground-value at from 18 to 20 years' purchase and *after* the rise at from 18 to 21 years' purchase, considering that the extra security is almost compensated for by the thirty or forty years which must have run off the lease before such a rise in ground-value could have occurred.

other conditions of the problem, that the buildings erected by B were of the annual value (apart from the site) of £2,500 instead of £500, in which case the premium paid by C for a lease at £500 per annum would be proportionately augmented. Now in this latter case the effect of a rise of £400 per annum in the value of the land would be to increase B's margin of security from £2,100 to £2,500 per annum, an increase that would obviously have quite an inappreciable influence on the capital value of B's secured rent. And yet in this case, as in the former one, the whole rates on the whole £400 a year would be thrown upon B's shoulders, while the whole increase of income would go unrated to C.

Now, no other attempt whatever has been made by Mr. Moulton to deal with my central position, that increase in "*ground-value*" (as defined in his pamphlet) is received by the persons entitled to the possession or to the receipt of the ultimate or rack rentals of the house and ground, not by the persons who receive a *fixed* annual payment for what *was* the value. But until that position is shown to be untenable, it can never be fair, in respect of an increase which goes into the pocket of the owner of the rack-rent, to rate the owner of a fixed rent because the capital value of his property is increased to some indefinite extent having no relation to the burden sought to be cast on him.

Mr. Moulton lays great stress in his reply on the well-known doctrine that it is useless to attempt to rate directly the rent representing the cost of a structure, or "building-"rent," because the builder will cease to build until rents have risen to such a point as to enable him to throw the rates in respect of the manufactured article (the house) on to the consumer—that is, the occupier. But it is strange that he does not see that, in the instance in question between us, B's rent of £400, which he proposes to rate, *is* a "building-rent," though it has by the increase in ground-values been brought within the ground-value for the time being. This rent is a part of B's remuneration for building the house just as much as the premium which C pays him. And if this rent is subjected, as Mr. Moulton proposes, to prospective local taxation on every increase of ground-value, builders will in future, on his own showing, throw on occupiers, in the shape of rent, the estimated amount of this prospective rating just as surely as would be the case with present rates.

To a merely personal question that arises between Mr. Moulton and myself I shall devote but two sentences. Mr. Moulton accuses me of having (not of malice prepense, but only from "inaccuracy of mind too habitual to be "conscious") entirely misrepresented upon an important point the views of John Stuart Mill, which, he asserts, are to the "very opposite effect." It is unpleasant to have to meet assertion by assertion in a matter of this kind, and I can only ask readers unused to Mr. Moulton's methods of controversy to carefully peruse the passage in question, bearing in mind the difference between (1) "annual value" or "rack-rent," (2) ground-rent as used by Mill, and (3) "value of the ground" or "ground-value" as used by Mr. Moulton, and then to decide which of us is the more accurate in his statement.

The really material and important point, however, for persons interested in the question to grasp is this, that, assuming all Mr. Moulton's premises, his proposals would entirely fail of the effect he desires in the following two ways. First, they would rate, not the recipients of the increase of ground-value, but the recipients of fixed rents, not the rents *created*, but only those *maintained*. And secondly, they would, as ground-values rise, rate those very building-rents which Mr. Moulton considers it of no use to rate at all, but which do, in fact, come next in order of succession to the original ground-rents and so would be first brought within the range of ground-values. In fact, the scheme is founded on an entire misapprehension and mistake; and the only wonder is that a United Committee for Advocating the Taxation of Ground Rents and Values should, after several years' existence, have nothing better to put forward than a proposal of this kind, the effect of which would be merely *to rate the wrong man*.

www.ingramcontent.com/pod-product-compliance
Lightning Source LLC
Chambersburg PA
CBHW030253170426
43202CB00009B/724